Rethinking

and the beliefs that guide you

Peter Teuscher

Copyright © 2024 Peter Teuscher

All rights reserved.

This book was edited by Chris Sowers and Wendy Hall

Cover Design by Anja von Puttkamer and Sarah Francke

ISBN: 978-3-00-076691-6

To Robert
who may or may not have inspired many aspects of this book

CONTENTS

INTRODUCTION

"I needed to write, to express myself through written language not only so that others might hear me but so that I could hear myself."
- Dr. Gabor Maté -

I'm looking into the eyes of a child. From his photograph, he looks to be a young boy about three years old. He is wearing a big smile and there is laughter in his eyes. Unfortunately, the happiness portrayed in this photo will not last. He will experience many things that will lead to self-doubt, confusion, and despair. He will experience depression and anxiety and begin to live with many fears. He will begin to believe many things about himself and the world that do not serve him. This will impact his choices and behaviours. The relationships he will have, his experiences at school, and everything he tries to be successful at, will be negatively impacted by his beliefs and his mental state. Most chances at success and happiness will elude him.

This child's story is familiar to me because the boy in the picture is me. As I look at the photo, my therapist asks me to tell the boy a different story about himself. We start with a core belief, which is a fundamental idea or deeply held belief that we may have about ourselves, others, and the world around us. Mine is one of several that have stood in the way of success and happiness and undermined me and my younger self for so many years. I have tried numerous forms of

1

therapy, which helped me change many of the core beliefs that did not serve me. Not everyone needs therapy to change; many beliefs do not require therapy to find a resolution. There are various ways to approach the beliefs we harbour in our conscious and unconscious minds. You will find my suggestions as you read on.

In 2001, after a lot of therapy and personal development work, I travelled through Europe, where I celebrated New Year's Eve in Berlin. As I often do around this time of year, I took time to reflect on the year gone by. After the tremendous growth and newfound clarity I had found in the previous months and years, I felt I had arrived. To start the new year, I attempted to summarise what I had learned in a few short lines. I wrote down the following words, which I would later share in an email to my friends.

We enter each New Year with unlimited possibilities, and the choices we make will either lead us closer to or further from where we want to be. Once we realize that, for the most part, we create our own problems and solutions, then we can hold ourselves accountable instead of making excuses. It is all about choices. Choosing to take control or give it. Choosing to be a victim or a victor. In the end, if you follow your heart, it will always lead you to where you need to be. . . happiness.

This message was important to me because it marked a clear change in my thinking and how I viewed the world. As much as I hoped it would inspire others, I wanted to challenge myself to articulate my ideas in a way that would help me curate a system of beliefs that would keep me on this path of growth, change, and greater happiness. I was beginning to realize that the new beliefs I had adopted were at the centre of all my positive changes and newfound happiness. However, back then, I was still closer to the beginning of my journey of personal development, and I now realize there is no arrival. Ideally, life continues to challenge us to learn and grow indefinitely.

Awareness allows change! This motto has accompanied me since the early days of my coaching practice. How can we uncover or bring to the surface the many beliefs that drive our behaviours, inform our strategies, and influence how we see the world? In addition to the variety of therapies I have participated in, there are many other ways I have pursued my personal development in an effort to be more self-aware and better understand myself. This was a spiritual journey, and although I did not adopt a particular religion, I did open my mind to ideas I had previously ignored or even ridiculed.

Over the years, my beliefs have evolved, and I have attempted to communicate these ideas in different ways, including an early attempt at writing a book. Having further developed and practiced those ideas, I have now captured them in this book. I continue to review and refine these concepts as I continue to evolve. Sharing these ideas with others and writing them down helps me better anchor them in my mind. It helps me to better live these ideas and not just talk about them. Hopefully, you will also benefit from reading them.

My purpose in coaching is to help people find their highest potential. This book is written with the same intention, whether in experiencing happiness or any other measure of success in life. Psychiatrist and author Dr. Iain McGilchrist has said it's a huge mistake in psychiatry to tell people what to do. Only when people become aware of why they are suffering can they realize what they need to do to change. I take a similar approach in coaching and in this book. There are no rules to life or instructions on what you must do in what I have to offer. I share the ideas of many great thinkers, along with my own, within the context that I have considered them. This is not a call to adopt my philosophy. When sharing my beliefs, I am trying to give context that will help others see how changes in belief can change one's life. I am not a guru or spiritual teacher, but an observer of life who is trying to help others become better observers of their own life.

Finally, the five ingredients I consider necessary to live a fulfilling life, which to me is a key ingredient to happiness, would be as follows. **Curiosity**, as without this quality, we will fail to try new things and ask challenging questions. **Desire**, as I believe in the benefits of being pulled toward something rather than being pushed or trying to avoid what we don't want. An **open mind** allows us to consider new options and avoid dogmatic thinking. **Determination** is the grit to pursue our desires regardless of setbacks. **Clarity of purpose** can drive our desire and keep us focussed on what is important. These ingredients have gone into the writing of this book, and perhaps they will serve you in your aspirations for change as you read on.

You may ask what happened to the boy in the photo. He decided to open his mind. He now recognizes that he is worthy and lovable. The man I have become continues to grow and evolve. The man I used to be no longer exists, to the point that many of my distant memories seem completely foreign to me. The physical and mental versions of myself have been replaced by new cells and new thoughts, while the spiritual part of me has been allowed to grow and flourish. Please don't misunderstand. I am not going to promote a particular religion or philosophy. If this book serves its purpose, and you desire it, any kind of change you seek is possible.

No secrets are revealed in this book, but it will lead to unlocking some secrets inside you. It is a journey worth taking. Of these two things I am certain. Thank you for choosing to let my words and ideas accompany you on this journey.

1 CONSIDERING HAPPINESS

"Happiness is different from pleasure. Happiness has something to do with struggling and enduring and accomplishing."
- George A. Sheehan -

The importance of happiness

It seems that beyond the most basic necessities in life, what is most sought-after in this world is happiness. Although we may have different names for it, the desire for happiness is something we all have in common despite differences in culture, religion, and politics. However, there are varying ways in which we define happiness or seek to be happy, whether consciously or unconsciously. Many do not even know what will make them happy and find themselves perpetually in pursuit of happiness. Meanwhile, others undermine or sabotage their happiness without realizing it due to erroneous beliefs and dysfunctional strategies for navigating life. Some may not even call it happiness but instead refer to this state as fulfillment, satisfaction, or success. Whatever you call happiness, we all strive, hope, or long for it in some way.

Some may consider the pursuit of personal happiness a selfish priority. After all, our world faces many challenges which seem to be of greater importance than the luxury of individual happiness. Encouraging people to live happier lives can, however, have positive effects on the world as well. According to my definition of happiness, happy people don't usually engage in such things as starting wars, oppressing people, or mistreating animals. They don't ruin their lives and others through the abuse of drugs and alcohol or obsessive behaviour. They are commonly better parents, neighbours, and citizens. When people have found ways to be authentically happy, they are often in a far better position to help themselves and others. For these reasons, I have a vested interest in encouraging people to seek out what makes them happy.

His Holiness the Dalai Lama has stated that the very purpose of life is to seek happiness. However, some would disagree. Some consider aspirations of happiness as frivolous, preferring loftier ambitions in life. For example, clinical psychologist and author Jordan Peterson discourages making happiness a measure of the quality of your life because positive emotion makes people impulsive. He also reminds us that happiness is fleeting, so we should not focus on it. I agree that all moments of joy, excitement, and accomplishment are fleeting, but is happiness not also the sensation that we experience when we pursue the work we are passionate about? Is an accomplishment worth as much to you if you do not feel any joy in its achievement?

Furthermore, is happiness not the feeling we have when we are enjoying time with those we love or when we are able to share something of value with others? When we overcome great challenges, do we not feel happy? Psychologist and author Mihaly Csikszentmihalyi of the groundbreaking book *Flow* points to this in his writing. Csikszentmihalyi has observed the connection between finding happiness in the things we do and what he refers to as the flow state. This demonstrates a connection between happiness and being the best version of ourselves.

Happiness is far more than just what you do in life. What about experiencing a beautiful sunset or hearing music that moves you? I see nothing wrong with striving to achieve as many such moments as possible. To say it is not worth aspiring to because it is fleeting is like telling someone not to raise their expectations or be hopeful because they could be disappointed. Every aspiration brings the risk of failure, and all things in life are temporary. I agree with Dr. Peterson that happiness is a byproduct, although he refers to it as a side effect. However, I feel it is a valuable indicator of the quality of our lives because it is some of the most relevant feedback life gives us regarding our thoughts, beliefs, and choices.

Thus we see the difficulties created by the meaning we give words or our interpretation of them. Happiness is simply a word meant to represent something intangible and is open to interpretation, like all words. I am not a social scientist or psychotherapist, but even if I were, I could not define happiness to suit everyone. No one can. This doesn't mean that you cannot define it for yourself. This is what I encourage people to do.

Since our assumptions, expectations, and perceptions—which are all associated with our beliefs—often stand in the way of our happiness, my recommendation is that you review and reassess your beliefs to help you find your own happiness. This is the primary intention of this book—to help you become more aware and consciously develop beliefs that allow happiness. I also encourage you to be clear on the meaning of the key words you use to define your core beliefs. Language is important.

Happiness is a state, not a destination, so I agree that pursuing it as a goal makes little sense. Most people I point this out to will nod in agreement, and yet somewhere hiding within their personal philosophy will be a belief telling them that if or when a certain thing happens, they will be happy. Those who consciously make happiness a goal will often find it just out of reach because their happiness is conditional and somehow reliant on circumstances and expectations lining up in perfect synchronicity. Then after those brief moments when their goal is achieved, they do not enjoy it long before chasing the next thing to make them happy. This is the crux of most people's ideas about happiness.

No matter how successful you are at creating the life you want in the external world, happiness is an inside job. As you look to define it, look within yourself. As you interact with the outside world, you will grow and learn, or you may fight and struggle, but you will experience life in your own unique way. The meaning you give to it will be found in your beliefs, which is why your beliefs are the key to your happiness.

Happiness is a sense of joy and fulfillment I experience through connection to others, nature, and myself. It is also what I experience through growth, learning, a sense of purpose, and adding value to the lives of others. I can maintain this state by managing my thoughts, beliefs, and physical well-being in the many ways I will describe throughout this book. These examples may help you identify what happiness means to you and how to experience more of it.

I used to confuse happiness with simply feeling good, but many things can trigger the reward centre in the brain to generate good feelings. Indulging in food, sex, drugs, gambling, shopping, and many other pleasures, which create temporary positive feelings, can all feel wonderful. Even negative acts like revenge or domination can generate a sense of power that feels good for a moment. However, none of these can be maintained, no matter how much time, money, or opportunities you have to pursue these experiences. Eventually, the thrill and excitement will fade, and thus the good feeling will be fleeting.

Authentic happiness can persist independently of external circumstances. This is a good starting point when determining what happiness means to you and what helps you experience more of it. You can start by considering the conditions under which you think you feel happy. From there, you can ask yourself, "Is this really happiness?"

With this in mind, by all means, set goals for yourself, but don't make happiness one of them. It is too vague to be a goal and too precious to be exclusively allocated to milestones you set for yourself. Life is one big feedback loop, and your level of happiness is an indication of the quality of your life. Many things contribute to this, from what you believe to the choices you make and the relationships you have. When you are dissatisfied with the level of happiness you experience, this is a good indication that it is time for you to re-examine all of the things that contribute to your happiness or lack thereof. The feeling of being happy can therefore be like the magnetic North on a compass; it can guide your direction in life.

I do feel that there are tremendous benefits to being happy, or in other words, filling your life with as many moments of happiness as you can. This doesn't mean there is anything wrong with feeling sad or any of the other emotions on the spectrum. I want to be clear that I am not constantly happy, nor is there an expectation that someone should be in every moment. Happiness comes in the present, and moments come and go. Without the lows that accompany the highs, we don't have the contrast to sort out what is important and what makes us happy. It is difficult to recognize and appreciate happiness if we are not familiar with sadness, anger, and despair. Therefore, these highs and lows are important in every life and are not meant to be circumvented. That said, spending as much time as possible in a happy state will positively impact everything, from the choices you make to how healthy you are.

Defining happiness
The first lines in the first verse of the Tao Te Ching state, "A way that can be walked is not The Way. A name that can be named is not The Name." This points to the undefinable nature of the Tao, which

translates to the way or the path. It helps us understand that sometimes our efforts to translate concepts into words or apply labels can diminish or limit them. There are a number of words that I will seek to define, but I do this to point toward an idea rather than limiting what it can mean for anyone else. This is the double-edged sword of creating definitions. It is both limiting and clarifying. By defining something, we naturally exclude what is not and create limits for what can be. These are the trade-offs of language.

That said, I do encourage people to define happiness for themselves. Or rather, I encourage people to better understand what conditions contribute positively or negatively to their state of happiness. I will provide many of my own definitions and highlight questions that I ask myself to keep me in line with what I have learned makes me happy.

Happiness is not black or white. In other words, we may not be either happy or unhappy, but we feel an array of emotions reflecting some degree of happiness we are experiencing. Just as people are not satisfied to simply stop feeling sad or depressed but would also like to experience some degree of happiness, there are many words to describe the various states with which we can associate feeling happy. For example, joy, amusement, excitement, wonder, and ecstasy can all be associated with happiness, but so can a sense of relief, gratitude, and compassion.

I remember a conversation with my nephew a few years ago where he told me how playing his Xbox video games made him happy. I tried to tell him about the chemical reaction the games were triggering in his mind that gave him the feeling he experienced. His confused look reminded me that this was not the way to discuss authentic happiness with a boy or anyone unfamiliar with neuroscience. It's true that good feelings are the result of chemicals in the brain, and some things very deliberately trigger this response, like reaching the next level in a video game. It could also be shopping, gambling, or overcoming a challenge. While there is nothing wrong with enjoying pleasurable moments, these are temporary, and people often live their lives striving for these highlights while treating everything in between these peaks as filler. These peaks are not how I define happiness.

Perhaps there was a time when life was only about survival or simpler times when happiness was not so elusive. We cannot relive the thoughts and feelings of our ancestors as if they were our own, but clearly, it is no longer enough for humans to survive and feel safe. We need meaning, purpose, and connection. It is part of our evolution. Unfortunately, in lieu of these things, we chase brief moments of satisfaction. Maybe you post things on social media and feel good when you get a lot of likes or positive comments. Maybe you play video games that stimulate the brain's pleasure or reward centre when you win. Or maybe you eat comfort food.

There is a name for the happiness derived from those fleeting moments of pleasure: hedonic happiness. This also refers to the sense we get from avoiding pain and suffering. However, there is another kind of happiness called eudaemonic happiness. This is based on the sensations derived from senses of meaning, purpose, and self-realization. If you rely on chemical reactions in your brain for your happiness, you will be very reliant on your environment and manipulated by the pleasure-seeking habits that you have developed. If you want to be in control of your happiness, the way you see the world will need some adjustment.

So often, I find that some people pursue an idea of happiness that will never fulfill them. This leads many to frustration and unhappiness. Developing a sense of what makes us happy and what gives our life meaning is essential in living a purposeful and self-aware life. I am not asking you to define happiness per se; I am recommending that you understand what it means for you to be happy. This may seem like a subtle difference, but from there, you can better understand all the factors that contribute to this state so you can find an abundance of happiness.

The more I see people striving for what they call happiness, the more I consider what society thinks is happiness to really be something else. Society has implicitly given us a checklist of things we should do with the unspoken promise that it will make us happy. Go to school and get good grades. Get a good job, work hard, get a promotion, and earn a lot of money so we can afford all the nice things in life. Find a partner and raise a family. There is nothing wrong with any of these aspirations in life, but none can guarantee happiness. Many people I have coached are disappointed because they have done everything they were recommended to do in life but are still not happy. It is unhelpful to let other people tell you what happiness is or how to achieve it. Again, it's an inside job, and only you can define it for yourself.

I do find it helpful to focus on what makes me happy rather than trying to define happiness itself. Feeling a sense of purpose and accomplishment or contributing to others or society makes me happy. This re-emphasizes that happiness is not a destination or a goal in life. Perhaps happiness is only the emotional guidance to let us know when we are aligned with our values, purpose, and abilities. Maybe happiness is the byproduct of a meaningful life—a life that has meaning to us regardless of what others think.

Happiness can be found in the simplest moments. For me, it can be the warmth of the sun's rays on a spring day or the joyful greeting of my dog when I return home from a trip. Peaceful moments in nature, deep conversations with close friends, learning something new, and overcoming a great challenge all generate happiness in me. So does looking at a piece of art or listening to beautiful music. How these things make me feel is not identical, but they are all some form of happiness. A long list of situations contribute to my happiness, but those external conditions are not responsible for how I feel. I have had all these things before and could not appreciate them or feel happy. They were moments of disappointment, anger, self-pity, and depression. They were times when my perception of the world and my reaction to its interpretation caused me to focus on the negative and react in ways that contributed to poor choices and negative emotions.

When I ask someone to explain their idea of happiness, they often define the conditions that contribute to feeling good. They may describe the sensation that reflects their mental state in particular moments, but when asked to be specific most people agree that it is just a feeling. Perhaps the biggest misunderstanding about happiness, as far as I can tell, seems to be the idea that happiness is contingent upon external circumstances. Sure, the external world can contribute to our mental state by making it more or less challenging to be happy. But the art of authentic happiness is to find happiness independent of what is going on around you.

In his book, *Man's Search for Meaning,* Viktor Frankl describes brief moments of happiness despite living in the horrific conditions of a concentration camp during the Second World War. He describes how he found meaning despite his suffering. Compare this to successful people, with all the comforts money can buy but are miserable, and it becomes easy to see that external conditions do not dictate happiness.

To help guide your own definition of happiness, I recommend some of the advice of ancient Greek philosopher Epicurus. He spent a great deal of his time trying to understand what makes people happy. He noticed that people expect happiness to come from their romantic relationships, wealth, and luxury, but concluded that what really makes people happy is very different. He defined three important elements of his approach to happiness: a combination of quality friendships, living a self-directed life, and finding inner calm. While the first two are tied to external conditions, one would think that the third is not. After all, inner calm by its very name seems to exclude outer circumstances. And yet inner calm is something many people try to achieve by first achieving a calm outer world. They try to control conditions by pursuing luxury and security.

Some people act as if the physical pleasures in life create the happiness they desire, but as Epicurus points out, this is not the case. Usually, the pleasures and comforts we seek are just to distract us from our fears and the suffering we create for ourselves. It is often the pursuit of our fear-based ambitions and primal desires that causes a great deal of frustration, disappointment, and suffering in life. It is when we tend to important relationships in our lives, cultivate a sense of purpose, and generate peace of mind independent of external conditions that we consistently experience happiness. This was Epicurus' philosophy on happiness.

In Buddhism, what could be referred to as happiness are the four factors of fulfillment. These are wealth, worldly satisfaction, spirituality, and enlightenment. Again, we have four very broadly defined terms open to interpretation. For example, what is wealth? For some, it is money and assets, but for me, one is not truly wealthy without knowledge and relationships. I consider my brother very wealthy, although he is middle-class by normal social standards. Most people who are middle class don't consider themselves wealthy, but what do you call someone who is in good health, with a beautiful, healthy family, a network of good friends, enough free time to enjoy life, and enough financial means to live well? I call such a person extremely wealthy.

Some people are content to pursue only the first two factors of fulfillment. Once they have a comfortable level of wealth and worldly satisfaction, they may not feel the need to pursue spirituality and enlightenment. This would not work for me. I cannot imagine a life where I am not continuously growing and evolving. A life of routine and comfort does not provide all I need for authentic happiness.

These are all examples of the way others have tried to define happiness. Whether you look to ancient philosophies or modern-day self-help gurus, no one can give you the definition of happiness that will best work for you. You can look to these for inspiration as I have, but it is best to develop your own meaning for the word to be successful at finding your happiness. Know what it means for you to be happy, and the life you lead will be simpler and more straightforward.

Finding your own way

In my life, I have taken both easier and more difficult paths in my search for happiness, and it is only in looking back that I realize just how far I have come. As Zen Master and Buddhist monk Thích Nhất Hạnh has said, there is no way to happiness. Happiness is the way.

Once you have defined what happiness means to you, it will make it easier to discover the kind of life that makes you happy. Then it is up to you to begin creating that life—creating that happiness for yourself. Like meditation, diet, and keeping fit, it is a matter of practice.

I am also not proposing anyone strive for a constant Brave New World kind of happiness. This Soma-induced happiness portrayed in the Aldous Huxley novel is often what we strive for as we pursue dopamine-inducing activities and rewards. We need contrast in life, both to appreciate what happiness is and to allow us to discern, make choices, and grow from these experiences. Only then can we truly appreciate the joy and satisfaction moments of authentic happiness can bring.

When asking someone what would make them happy, there are people who would tell you it would be winning the lottery and then retiring to a tropical beach drinking fancy little umbrella drinks. Honestly, how long would that make anyone happy? Instead, you can ask yourself if you would rather have a comfortable life or an interesting life. Personally, I would not trade any of my challenges or struggles for an easier life. Although I have had my share of frustrations, everything I have been through has made me who I am today, and I am happy with who I am now. So what does that tell you? Again, it tells you that happiness is not about the external world. It is an inside job.

Happiness is a product of the way you live your life. It is up to you to understand the kind of life that makes you happy. The kind of questions to be asking yourself are:

- What fulfills me?
- How can I find purpose in my life?
- Do I have a gift to give the world?
- What contribution can I make to my community?
- What positive impact can I make on others?
- How can I grow?
- What do I want to learn and experience?
- What emotional healing do I need, and what issues do I need to resolve to allow me to experience more happiness?

Throughout this book, I am simply trying to raise your awareness because awareness allows change. Life is a journey of discovery, but you will never really discover what makes you happy if you do not find your own way of living. I will continue to ask questions that I have asked myself over the years. They are questions about what you think and how you feel, which you may not have asked or not fully considered. Unfortunately, we are often directly or indirectly told what to think and feel, which is not the path to authentic happiness.

One of my mentors, Dr. Jonni Gray, once told me that you cannot change people; you can only give them the best example possible. My examples are provided in this book, but there are plenty of examples to take note of all around us. Economists have been measuring happiness for more than forty years. Denmark has been on or near the top of the list of countries ranked as happiest for that entire time. So you can take examples from Denmark, but as Danish author Malene Rydahl points out in her book, *Happy as a Dane*, what makes people in her country happy are common values. These are not values exclusive to Danes, but perhaps their culture implements them most effectively. The values she points out are trust, the freedom to be you, and finding purpose. While backpacking through Asia, I found many people who seemed very happy despite having little wealth by Western standards. For some, perhaps, this resulted from their cultural values, such as a belief in Karma, or as Nietzsche called it, *amor fati*, a love of one's fate.

Whether you take from the examples of Danish, Indian, or another culture, I encourage you to take the examples that resonate with you to help develop beliefs that support your happiness. Assemble these beliefs into a philosophy, and when you have created a philosophy that supports you without compromise and live it every moment of your life, you have become a master. Every step you take toward mastery is a step toward greater fulfillment and abundance in your life. Take the step and enjoy the journey.

I have posed some questions at the end of almost every chapter. You don't need to have the answers immediately, but even if you do, take your time with these questions. I suggest you use them as a prompt to further contemplate the ideas and possibilities this book offers.

Questions
- How do you define happiness?
- How much happiness do you experience in daily life? None? Very little? A moderate amount? A lot? Constant joy?
- In what situations do you feel happy?
- Do you know what makes you happy?

2 BELIEFS

"What then may guide a man? One thing and this only: philosophy."
- Marcus Aurelius -

The importance of a personal philosophy

Do you consider yourself a philosopher? Most people I ask do not. Yet from the time you could think, you have been accumulating beliefs about the world, your life, and your place in it. The sum of all these beliefs is what I consider an individual's philosophy. The main difference between a philosopher and the average person's beliefs is that the philosopher will have reflected and critically thought through their beliefs rather than accepting things at face value or making assumptions without careful consideration. I encourage you to become a philosopher, reviewing and reflecting on your most important beliefs to determine which support you in creating a happy life.

An individual's beliefs will inevitably influence all the decisions and behaviours of that person in fundamental ways. Defining a clear set of beliefs, which I continue to review and reflect on based on their utility and impact on my life, has been extremely practical and allowed me to thrive in ways I previously never thought possible. Consciously defining your life philosophy will change how you see and react to the world. It will positively influence the choices you make as well as the results you achieve. Without negative beliefs to undermine you or stand in your way, life will flow with less inner resistance. In doing so, the level of happiness and degree of satisfaction in the way you experience your life will grow significantly.

I once read a Morgan Wootten book on coaching basketball. He begins by stating that the first step to becoming a good coach is having a solid philosophy. "Without a philosophy, you will lack the road map and the directions necessary to achieve your goals," writes Mr. Wootten. The same is true of life. Without a clearly defined personal philosophy, we may find ourselves racing through life, lacking direction, insight, or a clear idea of what we are trying to achieve beyond surviving and accumulating the things we desire.

Most people already have bits and pieces of a philosophy which developed since they were old enough to think. I am referring to the beliefs we assemble from experience as we progress along life's journey. These provide the foundation for our choices, thoughts, and behaviours. In other words, whether or not you are aware of them, these beliefs are your philosophy.

For many of us, beliefs are rules we have made up for our own game of life, which can be limiting and rigid. Instead, I prefer principles that guide and support you, helping you avoid choices made due to negative thinking habits or the expectations of others. It is a process of discovering who you are to determine what you want. The answers are within all of us; as we discover them, it is helpful to incorporate them into a philosophy to have them easily accessible for every challenge we face and every choice we make.

How your beliefs define you

How each of us lives is dominated by our beliefs. This includes how well we fit into or are excluded from the society we live in. We pay attention to the segregation of people by visible attributes such as race, but far more segregation, often self-imposed, is done based on cultural or religious beliefs. Certainly, economic status and education play an important role in the social groups we interact with, but even then, belief plays a role. The fundamental beliefs around money and what is possible in life often set apart those who are successful and those who are not because these beliefs play a significant role in our choices and actions.

There is no limit to the areas of life impacted by beliefs. For example, if you have ever pushed your body beyond what you thought possible, you will understand how beliefs can help and hinder your athletic performance. A perfect example is the often-cited moment when Roger Bannister became the first person to run a mile in under four minutes. At that time, it was believed that it could not be done. And yet, on May 6, 1954, Bannister became the first man in history to set this precedent. Interestingly, within weeks of this accomplishment, Bannister's record was broken. Before this, it was widely believed that running a mile in less than four minutes was physically impossible.

Beliefs can set limits or create limitless possibilities. If you reflect on your life, you will surely remember moments that shaped your future and changed the way you saw the world. It is easy to think that our experiences define us, but it is the way we interpret those experiences and the beliefs we develop from them that plays a significant role in defining who we are and the choices we make. This is especially true of experiences we had as children. The way we interpreted our parents' words or actions may have led us to believe we are not loveable or good enough. Experiences at school may have led you to come to conclusions about your intelligence or level of ability. You may have made assumptions about your place in society based on interactions with your peer group. Most of all, the traumas or challenges you faced will have led to fearful beliefs about how to navigate life. All of these beliefs have defined you. Or rather, this is how you have defined yourself.

The reality of beliefs

*"Is there any knowledge in the world which is so certain
that no reasonable man could doubt it?"*
- Bertrand Russell -

A belief is any idea, concept, or habitual thought pattern that influences our perception of reality and our responses to it. They are often the stories we tell ourselves, and each other, which create our perception of reality.

Nietzsche did not believe in absolute truth and thus concluded that an objective truth about anything, including the meaning of life, was not possible. He observed that an individual is always limited in their experience of the world and their perception of it. That is not to say that he rejected truth completely. However, rather than seeing truth in correlation with reality, he considered truth a position from which one could orient oneself in the world.

Facts may inform some of our beliefs, but facts are open to interpretation. Scientists work with facts yet have conflicting theories, assumptions, and biases about every topic under the sun. Beliefs are subjective by nature, and yet our entire world—the reality we operate in—is created out of beliefs in a fundamental way. Are concepts like democracy, national borders, laws, and money real? Are they not simply concepts and ideas we agree to accept as reality? They are beliefs by consensus that we have organized and enforced in some way. So many of the things we take for granted which allow our society to function only do so because all people, or at least the majority, believe in them.

Let's take the example of money. Do you realize that the bank notes you use for money are actually just promissory notes, in other words, debt? Most people do not know the history of money. The bank notes we call money have their origins in a time when debts were traded as currency. They only represent a promise to pay, and yet we believe those coins and slips of paper, or perhaps the digital currency you transfer between bank accounts, to have some intrinsic value. It would not be possible to use Deutsch marks, Italian lira, or French francs to pay for something in Europe today. European politicians in most European Union countries agreed on a single currency at the beginning of this century, making previously used currencies obsolete over time. Thus our monetary system is more a matter of organizing and controlling who gets what and may be volatile in its nature, as demonstrated in countries that experience hyperinflation, such as the Weimar Republic in the 1920s or, more recently, Venezuela and Zimbabwe. Money, or fiat currency, is based on a collective belief. And for many people, it influences happiness.

The monetary system is but one example of how beliefs create our reality. Our legal system and the notion of property ownership are human constructs most of us believe in. Human rights are a belief, not a naturally occurring phenomenon, and so are the particularities of the diverse cultures on the planet. Certainly, culture is built on traditions and habitual behaviours, but without a strong belief in these, they would soon fade into history.

What makes a person of authority powerful? Are kings and queens born with significantly different attributes or talents that ordinary people lack? No, it comes from a time when kings were believed to have a direct connection to God. How do you know if someone shouting from a podium knows how to lead or if one should obey someone in a position of authority? A great deal of power comes from convincing people to believe. So I ask you to consider again, is your reality influenced more by beliefs or facts?

I want to clarify that I in no way want to discount the importance of facts. Facts can help us recognize and overcome our cognitive biases as well as avoid irrational fears and superstitions. However, if we assume that we live in a fact-based reality and facts are unchangeable, our potential for change becomes more difficult. It is, therefore, important to recognize that we interpret facts and build beliefs around these interpretations, but we also build beliefs around ideas with only partial or no basis in fact. It is, therefore, important to recognize that we live in a world that has a far greater basis in belief than any of the facts that science has provided us.

Also, as much as science has been instrumental in understanding and manipulating our environment and improving many aspects of the quality of human existence, it does a poor job of helping us understand our inner experiences and therefore provides us with an incomplete truth. If someone close to you dies, their medical diagnosis or autopsy results will not help you deal with painful emotions. But in many ways, beliefs can. There is so much to know about our universe and life, and although we seek truth and look for proof in facts, our reality revolves around or is reflected in our beliefs, regardless of truth or facts.

We live in a world where truth is not always obvious. Facts and information from a multitude of sources around us every day try to convince us of their truth, making it increasingly difficult for individuals to determine what is true for them. I find it important for people to find their own truth because I witness people all the time trying to live in an ideological framework that has been constructed by others, which neither helps them be successful nor allows them to be happy. Your truth comes from within, and as you continue to read, you will understand why I think this is so.

I point out the extent to which beliefs fundamentally define the world we live in to help emphasize the importance of digging into your own beliefs. If beliefs create so much of the external reality we live in, imagine how much individual beliefs determine everything—from personal success and happiness to health and well-being. I am proposing that the state of your life and the results you have achieved, good and bad, are largely due to what you believe.

Where your beliefs come from

Many of our beliefs were adopted from those closest to us in our early years until we grew old enough to challenge those beliefs, discard some of them, and adopt new ones for better or worse. Experiences from a very young age caused us to develop assumptions and strategies for dealing with our environment. We gave meaning to events based on our interpretation and emotional response to those situations. Many of these made sense at the time and might even have been appropriate for that age, but some no longer serve us in our present phase of life. You probably still carry with you some erroneous or limiting beliefs from earlier phases of your life. In many ways, your mind is programmed by a variety of influencing factors. Although I don't believe one has to understand where particular beliefs originated, it may be helpful to recognize the source of some of your beliefs to let go and adopt new, more helpful ones.

I use the following framework to look at the origin of my beliefs. It is a simple and very general model but continues to be helpful for me in my ongoing process of identifying unhelpful beliefs and attempting to change them.

Experience

In my philosophy, experience is the most important source of belief. We interpret our experiences and develop strategies to replicate outcomes or avoid them in the future. Our experiences can generate tremendous personal growth or lead to beliefs that will continually stand in the way of our progress. How we process, interpret, and revisit those experiences over time will influence how our beliefs evolve. The meaning we give events will create a feeling and an emotional response. The stronger this emotional response, the stronger our belief will be. We can reflect on past experiences to overcome fearful beliefs and develop new, more positive ones by recognizing that events have no meaning except the meaning we give them in our minds.

Think about early failures in your life or highly emotional negative experiences. Which beliefs did these lead to? I came to Canada when I was four years old. At that age, I would still sometimes wet the bed. In their frustration, my parents threatened to take me to the orphanage if I didn't stop this behaviour. Were my parents ready to abandon me? Did they not love me? No, they were young frustrated parents who didn't know how to cope with the situation. Yet for years, my adult relationships were plagued by behaviour based on a fear of abandonment and a sense that I was unlovable. The way I interpreted subsequent experiences in my childhood reinforced these beliefs.

If you were rejected by someone or bullied by some kids at school, if you failed at something and never tried it again, if you got the attention you wanted by performing crazy antics or given praise for certain behaviours—any of these could have led to beliefs that you still carry with you, for better or worse.

Environment

From the time we were born, we were surrounded by people and influences that helped mould our beliefs. The family we were born into came with conditions that defined our early environment. Our interactions with our parents, relatives, and others we were close to influenced early beliefs about ourselves and how we should act. This process continued with our teachers, friends, and role models. In childhood, many of our beliefs were adopted from these sources. They provided us with examples of behaviour, after which we may have modelled some of our own beliefs about how we should act and navigate the world. We may have been exposed to fear and violence or love and safety. All of this helped form our beliefs.

There are also social or cultural influences in our environment, and depending on our exposure to them, various forms of media also become a significant influence on what we believe. In my youth, television strongly influenced my generation, but today, young people are surely more influenced by social media. The culture we grow up in and the social norms we witness all contribute to what we believe.

We very quickly learn rules about the etiquette and behaviour demanded of us by society. The activities we witness in our environment may cause us to believe what is normal and what is not. Very quickly, we are programmed with many judgements and opinions about life. We have no reason to question it if we don't have any experience to contradict this programming. However, when we do encounter something contrary to what we have been taught to believe, it may confuse us. As a result, we either ignore our experience or are compelled to change what we believe.

As adults, we may become part of new peer groups and develop or change our social and political views. The conditions we work in, the neighbourhoods we live in, and the culture we are exposed to every day will change or reinforce beliefs about life and how to live it.

Repetitive thought
When you think a particular thought over and over again to the point that it is an automatic reaction, it has become a habit. It could then be surmised that habitual thoughts become beliefs. These thoughts can refer to any number of things, from foods you like or dislike to your ability to perform tasks or skills. You can develop a pattern of thinking about any idea or concept based on experience, fact, or fantasy.

Often we mirror or mimic the words and ideas we hear around us. As social animals, we desire to fit in and become part of the community. As we internalize these ideas by repeating them verbally and mentally, we adopt them as our own. If you find yourself in an environment such as school or the workplace and the people around you have negative attitudes and are constantly complaining, you may also find yourself thinking similar thoughts. If a complaining habit begins to take hold of your mental dialogue, you will begin to internally repeat what you hear externally. As you continue to think these thoughts, you will strengthen neural pathways in your brain that will generate similar thoughts, creating a network in your brain around a particular idea. With enough repetitive thought, these ideas will develop into a belief.

Of course, our thinking habits don't just come from our environment. We all have an inner narrator, and this inner dialogue can become very repetitive. Sometimes the topic is self-criticism or the judgement of others. We can see more examples of how we rationalize or justify our actions or those of others. They can also be very positive, telling us we did well or are strong enough to keep going. The more frequently we return to a train of thought, the stronger it becomes anchored in our minds, especially if we begin expressing or explaining it to others. These thoughts soon become habits and lead to the creation of beliefs.

A lie repeated often enough can become your truth. This is perhaps the most important point to remember as you review your current beliefs. This can be a lie you tell yourself or one repeated by external influences. If there ever was an expert in the process of convincing the masses to believe lies, it was Joseph Goebbels who was responsible for propaganda during Nazi Germany. Goebbels says, "A lie told once remains a lie, but a lie told a thousand times becomes the truth." I prefer the more positive example from American author Robert Collier. "One comes to believe whatever one repeats to oneself sufficiently often, whether the statement is true or false. It comes to be dominating thought in one's mind."

It is not necessary to know where your beliefs originated to change them. I have shared these ideas about the formation of beliefs because you can use the same process to adopt and internalize new beliefs. If negative experiences lead to limiting beliefs, seek new positive experiences to convince yourself of the opposite. Changing your environment can allow you to experience and interpret life in new and perhaps better ways. Taking steps to monitor and change the thoughts you frequently have can develop new, more positive beliefs. These ideas may help you as you read on.

Perception

"No facts exist; only interpretations."
- Friedrich Nietzsche -

We all have a lens through which we see the world, and the focus of this lens is adjusted by our beliefs. Essentially we see the world through the filter of our beliefs, which is one reason we all see the world in different ways, with some perceptions varying more than others. When I travel, I see how the cultural beliefs of people cause them to see the world much differently than the culture I was raised in. Neither of us is right or wrong; we simply have our truth based on the information available to us, the beliefs that influence our per-spective, and the experiences that led us to our conclusions.

Behavioural scientists have determined that whether a person is happy or unhappy is largely determined by their outlook. Of course, other social, material, and genetic factors play a role, but the way we see the world seems to be the most significant variable. Research has shown that once those needs required for survival have been fulfilled, the conditions of our life have very little to do with the level of satis-faction we experience. For example, a study from the University of Illinois indicated that the richest Americans with an annual income of more than ten million dollars expressed only marginally higher levels of happiness than those who worked for them. This, despite living significantly different lifestyles. Research done in Singapore by Professor William Tov considers how culture influences happiness. In particular, he has looked at differences in perception between Asian cultures and those of Europeans and Americans. The way we perceive the world seems to have a significant impact on our level of happiness.

There are almost infinite perspectives from which each person can experience the world. Consider being part of the audience of a live music performance or live theatre. The musicians or actors have a much different experience than the spectators, and each audience member has their own individual experience. They may be similar but still different. When I play basketball, my experience is much different from when I watch the game, and my experience as a spectator varies whether I am watching a game live or in person.

Perspective informs our beliefs, and our beliefs influence our perception. When I play basketball, I may start to believe that I am not a good shooter if I miss a few shots. If this belief persists and I make a difficult shot in the future, I may perceive it was just luck. When what we perceive leads to a belief, we will begin to see the world through this lens. It is this feedback loop, along with the variability of possible experiences, that contributes to such diversity in life.

Of our five physical senses, those who are not visually impaired rely most heavily on sight to determine what is real in the world, which then strongly influences their perception. Do you think seeing is believing? Do you believe you can see reality? If so, I encourage you to consider more closely the process by which we see it.

From our own experience, it could be easy to assume that we see things exactly as they are. However, we do not see like a camera. Instead, the eye sends signals through optic nerves to the visual cortex, where information is processed. For efficiency, the reticular activating system in the brain sorts out what it considers the important or relevant details and fills in the picture based on historical data already stored in the brain. What we see is the brain's interpretation of what is out there. It is a prediction rather than a precise replication. We are processing data and combining it with what we know or think we know, which creates our perception of the world in our minds. If we receive new information, it can change what we see. This can be demonstrated when looking at a type of optical illusion where an image is embedded within a design pattern. Often you will be prompted to see the image or someone will point it out, but once you see it, you can't unsee it. Your brain now knows it's there.

Your reticular activating system has been programmed by the same influences that programmed many of your beliefs. Therefore, the beliefs and conditioning from your past define the filter for what gets through. This is why I tell people that we see the world through the filter of our beliefs. This is an important system that helps us focus on information that is most relevant to us so that we are not overwhelmed by the massive amount of information available. It is a way for the brain to be discerning with the information it allows for processing. Unfortunately, if we have, for example, a lot of negative, fearful beliefs, the filter will let related information through, which causes us to only look at the negatives and the risks. If we want to see opportunities, we may need to change our beliefs and reprogram our filters.

It may also be that we remember things worse than they were, which informs our filters. The brain doesn't know the difference between what we have experienced and what we imagine having experienced. Our fears conjure many negative images about possible outcomes, and the more we imagine such outcomes, the more real they become to us. You can see how this can be very beneficial for keeping us safe, but taken too far, it can be extremely limiting and compromise our potential. In this way, neuroscience shows us that we do not make direct contact with the physical world. We only experience it through our nervous system. Thus the experiences we remember are an interpretation of what has happened.

There are notable differences in perception in some people, such as those with synesthesia. These people may blend their senses—

hearing sounds associated with certain colours, seeing numbers in different colours, or experiencing some other combination of visual, spacial, and auditory sensations. A more common example is that women generally see a wider range of colours than men or can at least distinguish more subtle distinctions in colour. Then there are people with a visual or hearing impairment whose other senses may become heightened. All of these can result in subtle or significant differences in the way an individual may experience the world or reality. They all contribute to the formation of beliefs, which in turn influences the way we see the world.

Our perception informs the meaning we give to experiences and situations. The meaning we give to these influences the development of beliefs. However, the meaning we have given something comes from the perspective from which we viewed an experience. Consider how your worldview might change if you lived immersed in a different culture for some time. A person who is racist and then experiences discrimination, a rich person experiencing poverty, or someone who has come close to death—all have experiences that change the way they see the world. Each one of us sees the world differently now than in our childhood or youth because, at least in part, experience has caused us to develop beliefs which affect the way we see the world. With this awareness, we can seek out experiences to broaden our view of the world or reflect on ways to see past experiences differently.

If you travel and explore other cultures, you may encounter people with perspectives that seem foreign to you. Their expectations and understanding of how life should be will doubtless be much different from your own, even if your basic desires to be happy, healthy, and loved are the same. If you have ever had a discussion with someone who had the opposite opinion on a topic like politics or religion, you may have been left bewildered by their view on life. Yet, in their eyes, you may seem abnormal. We live in a world of diversity, which provides a wonderful opportunity to reflect on how we see the world without judging others.

In many ways, how you see the world is a choice. Take the example of Einstein's profound question: "Do we live in a friendly or hostile universe?" By choosing to see the universe as friendly or hostile, each of us makes a choice about how to see and experience our world and the life we live. When you start to recognize that you can choose how to see things, you will also start to recognize that, in many ways, happiness is a choice—a choice we make through our beliefs and perceptions.

Developing new beliefs

There are three areas I focus on when helping others change their beliefs. They are: have new experiences, change your environment, and think new thoughts. Sometimes when we have a fear-based belief, it can be helpful to do something to overcome that fear. For example, if you fear public speaking, you could practise speaking in front of a small group and progress to larger groups. As you have new experiences, you will gain confidence and begin to change your belief tied to that fear. Second, it can be difficult to change negative beliefs if your environment continues to reinforce them. When I travelled through Asia and then moved to Europe, I began to reconsider some of my beliefs, but you don't need to move countries to change your beliefs. The place you work and live or the people you surround yourself with are parts of your environment to consider when reflecting on the beliefs that you want to change. Finally, beliefs can change by changing your thoughts, and I will explore this in more detail in a later chapter.

The most important thing to remember about beliefs is that you have a choice. Some people treat beliefs as though they are some involuntary characteristic of their personality. Granted, some new beliefs are more difficult to adopt than others, and I do not believe you can will yourself to suddenly believe something. It will take time, reflection, and evaluation. Even then, it can be difficult. It is because our beliefs are the foundation of our reality that we are so resistant to changing them. They have become so familiar and comfortable that they have established themselves as our truth. Our comfort zone can be difficult to break out of. This makes it uncomfortable to question our beliefs since this also means questioning our truth and our sense of reality.

In many ways, our beliefs also become part of our identity. This is true of, but certainly not limited to religious and political beliefs. I will discuss identity in a later chapter, but it is certainly difficult to let go of something that feels like part of you. When we give up part of our identity, we may feel lost and incomplete. For this reason, it is important to learn how to separate ourselves from our beliefs. We have all done this many times before when we transitioned from childhood into adults. Letting go of identification with certain ideas or beliefs will make adopting a new philosophy easier.

I realize some will find this process challenging, but I don't expect someone to go from being an atheist to a devout religious person. Besides, I see no benefit in changing this type of worldview unless it is negatively affecting a person. Since there are happy and successful atheists and happy and successful religious people, I assume this is not the key area we need to focus on. My intention is not to tell you what beliefs to change but rather to send you on a journey of self-reflection so you can discover this for yourself.

In his book *Peace is Every Step*, Thích Nhất Hạnh points out that many people go to therapy to get rid of painful feelings and to help process their emotions. He comments that people want to eliminate their pain but are unwilling to change their beliefs. I agree with him that beliefs are often the source of our problems and suffering.

People will hang on to their beliefs as a part of their identity, something that cannot be changed. If this is what you believe, this will be the first belief you need to change if you want to use the ideas in this book. Therapy, coaching, and other approaches to personal development can have life-changing effects on your belief system. It may not always be easy, but the benefits are tremendous.

Faith

A philosophy requires faith to be effective. Not faith in dogma or scripture, but in your ability to discern, reflect, and create a belief system that works for you. Throughout my life, I have been curious about the level of faith some people possess toward a religion, a political system, an organization, or even the human race. I have sometimes envied people who believe so passionately in their spiritual beliefs that none of their life experiences could diminish their faith. And yet I could not find the conviction to believe what they believed.

When I reflect on the many years I considered myself an atheist, I considered my beliefs to be based on facts and science, yet many of my beliefs were quite dogmatic. I believed in institutions and the systems operating all around me, not because I gained a clear understanding of these things. I had faith in many things without any proof. Believing in science or institutions can sometimes require as much faith as any spiritual belief. I now acknowledge this. When facts are available, I try to let them inform my beliefs. When there are no facts to guide me, I rely on my philosophy and my intuition. Sometimes I even believe in things without a factual basis because I recognize that they help me in some way.

Faith used to be a word that triggered negative judgements and emotions in me. Now I recognize that we all have faith in something. We go to bed having faith that the sun will come up again the next day and the world will be roughly the same as we left it. The trust we have in each other is a form of faith. So I am encouraging you to have some faith in your ability to reflect on ideas and to discern not only between those that make sense to you rationally but also those that serve your highest potential. If you see the utility in what you believe and it does not harm you or anyone else, then have faith in this belief. As you assemble these beliefs into a philosophy, have faith that this is the best possible perspective to view the world and make the most of your human experience. Gather evidence for yourself to determine if it is working for you, rather than letting others cast doubt on it.

Abraham Maslow didn't believe religion was based on truth but that it contained important truths about life. Having read about and explored a variety of religions, I tend to agree with him. The term "myth" has such negative connotations, but I believe we need our myths to help make sense of the world. In religion, some may confuse metaphorical truth with literal truth, which only becomes a problem when we try to impose our beliefs on others. Myths and metaphors can often provide a much better intuitive understanding of life than the cold hard facts provided by some academics. Philosophy, too, is often most helpful in those areas of life where there are no clear answers or proof.

Life is a feedback loop in which happiness is one form of feedback. The experiences we have and the feelings they generate in us will be the feedback we need to affirm that our philosophy is leading us in the right direction. The more positive this feedback is, the stronger our faith in this philosophy will be.

This book is intended to help you develop a high level of awareness about yourself and the world you live in. Being more self-aware will help you trust yourself and have faith in the beliefs you have developed. This faith in your personal philosophy will allow you to live it with confidence and conviction. If your philosophy supports your happiness and success, you will experience a great deal of happiness and success.

"If you wish to strive for peace of soul and pleasure, then believe;
if you wish to be a devotee of truth, then inquire."

Questions

- What are some things you believe that are not based on facts, i.e., you have no proof to substantiate your beliefs?
- Do these beliefs support your success and happiness? If so, how?
- How do you know you're right? In other words, why do you think that your beliefs are true?
- Do you have beliefs that you know stand in the way of your success and happiness? Are you willing to change them?

3 THE FOUNDATION

"I simply can't build my hopes on a foundation of confusion, misery and death. . .
I think. . .peace and tranquillity will return again."
- Anne Frank -

Over many years of defining, reviewing, and revising my personal philosophy, a few concepts have remained consistent. I didn't start creating my philosophy by sitting down and defining my core principles. Instead, they became apparent over time. These are now ideas that guide all other areas of my philosophy, which is why I consider them the foundation of my belief system.

You will surely also have some fundamental beliefs that guide your thoughts and actions, making this an important place to start as you try to define a philosophy that supports your success and happiness. If you hold core beliefs that undermine your potential, this will carry over into every other part of your life. For this reason, as you continue through the book, you can continue to become aware of your current foundational beliefs and determine whether they support you. If they are not clear, you can begin to consider which fundamental principles you want to live by.

What is reality? What is the meaning of life? What is the right way to live? These are some of the deep questions philosophy seeks to answer. Philosophers throughout history have defined their answers to these questions, and I challenge you to do the same.

Morality and ethics are at the core of many philosophies, which I think is important but not always a useful starting point. Ethics are woven throughout my philosophy, but I did not begin with a set of moral or ethical principles. Instead, I sought to create some principles to live by that were both practical and reflected my core values around morality. Without broad application, philosophy will be nothing but some lofty ideals that you aspire to but never really apply in everyday life.

In addition, morals stem from our core values. Core values tend to be universal, while beliefs are often contextual. Although your values can evolve over time through different phases of your life, they are not something you can consciously change and adapt in the way I am proposing you do with your beliefs.

All the beliefs in the book, whether they have come through my contemplation or the study of other philosophies, are those that I consider to bring out the best in me and help me live a happier life. They are not a prescription, rules, or scripture to be followed dogmatically. I am only pointing to the areas in my life that I have thought most deeply about and which I believe will be helpful for you to consider more closely. If done with a reasonable degree of self-awareness, I am confident that anyone can adopt and develop their own set of beliefs that support their success and happiness.

The following five concepts are fundamental elements of my philosophy. They create a basis for me to better understand myself, life, and the nature of reality. It is important that the concepts you ultimately choose as the foundation of your philosophy answer your deepest questions about life. The practical beliefs that apply to daily life are built on top of these. In my case, a foundation provides some guiding principles, and the rest of my philosophy is concerned with the application of these principles.

Consciousness

"If man had no eternal consciousness, what would life be but despair?"
- Soren Kierkegaard -

What is consciousness?

Consciousness is often identified as a state of awareness. It has been described as the ability to know what it is like to be something. However, we know that when we sleep or are somehow rendered "unconscious," our consciousness persists. How, then, do we define what consciousness is? Where does consciousness begin and end? Where does it come from and how does it arrive? Perhaps one day, science will have this clearly mapped out for us, or perhaps consciousness is so all-encompassing and complex that it will never be fully understood. For now, it may help us to define it for our own philosophies, so I will share what I understand of this concept.

With a mechanistic view of the universe, a reductionist approach to understanding life makes sense. If the universe, our planet, and our bodies are machines, it is logical to think we could break everything down to its simplest parts and then understand how they work. However, we live within complex systems that cannot be understood by looking only at their parts in isolation. Neuroscience has not been able to identify the self or the source of consciousness in the brain, so there is no way to understand consciousness by reducing it to its fundamental parts.

Many scientists believe in an emergent universe. The universe emerged from the Big Bang. Life emerged from the combining of elements on the planet. And finally, consciousness emerged within some of the creatures whose brains had evolved to support such qualities. If you believe that consciousness is an emergent property of the brain, you may find that no further consideration is required.

Therefore, a deeper examination of the concept will not be needed in your philosophy. Coming to this conclusion is, however, an important part of the process.

If you were trying to explain the world to an advanced computer system or some form of artificial intelligence, you might formulate this in terms and concepts as we do in science. Would this conceptual way of describing the world be enough for an AI to understand life? Can we share such experiences in a way that provides understanding? No matter how much we understand biology, we will not know what it is like to be a dog, horse, frog, or dolphin. Could an AI ever understand what it is like to be you?

This is where we fall short in scientific explanations of the world and consciousness. We try to create terminology and apply labels or classifications and theories to describe life, but can these ever be complete? Naturally, science is important, giving us a far better understanding of the mechanics and processes of the world around us, but does it give us a complete and holistic understanding of the world? According to mathematical physicist and philosopher of science Sir Roger Penrose, consciousness is not a computation because equations can not create understanding. This is why I feel it is important to consider consciousness from other perspectives.

Many ancient indigenous cultures have spiritual beliefs that describe a worldview now referred to as Animism. Animals, trees, bodies of water, and elements are assumed to have spirits or energy that could interact with people's lives. Although this may have been taken literally within those cultures that embraced these beliefs, for me, it tells a metaphorical truth about the interdependence of humans and the environment. It suggests that a form of consciousness is pervasive throughout nature.

The view that my original meditation teacher shared with me could be considered Pantheism. This is the view that God is everything or everything is God. A version of this ideology was also held by the famous Dutch philosopher Baruch Spinoza, who saw God as synonymous with nature. Spinoza believed everything exists in the mind of God. This is not to be confused with Panentheism which considers the divine to be present in everything or that it interacts with all of life. Therefore, since God is conscious, everything has some consciousness in it.

Italian philosopher Francesco Patrizi was the first to use the term panpsychism in the sixteenth century, but the concept was considered by philosophers even before the time of Socrates. Only in recent years have some physicists begun to consider panpsychism as a viable theory for considering the nature of the universe. The concept itself proposes that all things have a mind or a mind-like quality which would indicate that the mind is not limited to the brain, nor is a brain even necessary to have a mind. In fact, the brain does not have any special matter to make it conscious. As I understand it, panpsychism is then the belief that consciousness or mind is a universal feature or quality in all things.

I am not convinced by a mechanical or emergent view of the universe, so my view is far more in line with the panpsychists. I see no benefit in giving it a name, but I live by the principle that the universe is conscious and that existence or reality is a manifestation or product of the universe experiencing itself in infinite ways. My unique experience then contributes to the growth and evolution of universal consciousness. Furthermore, my interaction with reality and my impact on other expressions of consciousness have an effect on the whole. For this reason, individual experience is essential. I see each of us as focussed consciousness that manifests as an individual point of awareness. All that we are unaware of is not necessarily unconscious but simply outside our current awareness or individual experience.

If one imagines the sun or a star representing consciousness, I would consider each of us as a beam of light shining on and exposing potential experiences. I have also considered that we could be living in a matrix-like simulation. However, the simulation need not necessarily take place in some massive, highly advanced computer system. It could be that source consciousness is manifesting this reality, which allows us to have these conscious experiences. In this case, the circumstances would be very similar to Spinoza's view that we are living in the mind of God.

I encourage you to play with these ideas in a creative and open way. It may help you see beyond your current life experience, allowing you to consider new and empowering beliefs about the nature of reality. This line of thinking has helped me find more meaning and purpose in my life. Belief in this perspective contributes to a mental framework that clarifies how I want to live. Hopefully, you too will benefit from considering what consciousness means to you.

Why is consciousness important?
Whether you have thought deeply about the nature of consciousness and whether you have come to some conclusions, the following prompts may help you consider it more deeply. It may not be part of your foundational beliefs, but some well-defined beliefs around consciousness will impact the way you live life.

The question of consciousness continues to fascinate philosophers and puzzle neuroscientists, which is why most refer to it as the hard problem of consciousness. My definition is not so concrete that I could formulate a hypothesis or create a mental model for anyone to adopt. This is mainly because I do not think the human condition allows us to fully comprehend the nature of consciousness. However, what my definition points toward provides enough to guide my philosophy. In sharing this with you, I hope to provide a similar experience to one I had with my first mediation teacher. We did not discuss consciousness, but he did share his thoughts about God.

At the time, I was someone for whom this word God conjured all kinds of negative images. God, to me, was a fictional character. A bearded, white-haired, old man on a throne in the sky whose conceptual presence in religion or mythology had inspired the worst in humanity, including wars, persecution, and many other forms of violence. My meditation teacher provided me with an alternative way to consider God. One so different that it shifted my own perspective from that of an atheist to an agnostic. I could no longer be sure of any beliefs about religion and spirituality held to that point.

My teacher was an Indian man in Vancouver in 2000. Sadly I have forgotten his name, but he instructed me for two months in a form of meditation where I had to refrain from drinking alcohol or eating meat. I had recently stopped eating meat, but my brother and I had a craft brewery, so it would be difficult to give up alcohol indefinitely. I also had to promise not to teach anyone else the method or the mantras that I had learned. I eventually decided his teachings had too much of a religious element, so I did not continue that practice.

As mentioned, the most profound idea I took away from this teacher came from his concept of God. He asked me to imagine the universe as an ocean of energy. Each of us, he described, is a drop in that ocean, and the ocean is God. This image resonated with me so strongly and opened my mind so significantly that I could not stop thinking about all the possibilities. I began to believe there might be more to me than my physical body and the chemical reactions in my brain. He did this through a simple metaphor. For the first time, someone provided a picture of God that was not some bearded, grey-haired, old man who observed and judged me from a distance. This was not the patriarchal authority figure associated with the endless dogma that people had been trying to convince me of. I became curious and explored further.

As with all of my beliefs shared in this book, I decided to rethink my beliefs about spirituality when I realized that my negative thoughts and assumptions about religion and spirituality did not support me. I had made the assumption that science showed me all that I needed to know, and anyone who believed in the esoteric or lived life by a religion was superstitious, gullible, and in denial of reality out of fear of their mortality. My worldview prior to these experiences left me feeling alone because I was in the minority, surrounded by believers with a history of persecution that not so long ago included stoning, burning at the stake, or otherwise condemning non-believers. It also felt out of touch with the ethereal nature of being human. Simply said, my beliefs—or perhaps more accurately, my prejudice—with regard to spirituality did not support my happiness.

If consciousness is the ocean we exist in or are part of, this makes it impossible to observe and understand. No matter how much of the universe we can explore and observe, we can never observe the fullness of consciousness. When David Foster Wallace addressed the 2005 graduating class at Kenyon College, he began with this: "There are these two young fish swimming along, and they happen to meet an older fish swimming the other way, who nods at them and says 'Morning, boys. How's the water?' And the two young fish swim on for a bit, and then eventually one of them looks over at the other and goes, 'What the hell is water?'" Although I am not claiming he was referring to consciousness, it does help illustrate the difficulty in defining and quantifying something that is the fabric of our reality.

To return to the original question: why is consciousness important? Whether you take a scientific view or a more spiritual perspective, consciousness is the essence of who you are. What could be more important to developing a personal philosophy than defining the nature of consciousness for yourself?

How does consciousness impact a philosophy?

Consciousness is at the centre of all experience, so it is difficult not to give it some consideration when developing a personal philosophy. Perhaps then, the question is not if it should be considered but how it can be integrated into a belief system. This will, of course, depend on whether you believe that consciousness is an emergent property of the brain, an all-pervasive intelligence, or something else completely. The brief paragraphs in the previous section don't begin to scratch the surface of all that can be said about consciousness but will hopefully have provided a starting point for defining what consciousness means to you.

Consciousness can also be seen as more than one thing, or perhaps it can take different forms, the same way that water has different states. There are those elements of consciousness that are outside of our awareness which we often refer to as the unconscious or subconscious. In one respect, consciousness is simply the ability to be aware and have experiences. This defines what it means to be conscious in basic terms, but on a deeper level, consciousness may be the essence of all life.

How I define consciousness is at the core of my beliefs about spirituality and the nature of reality. Without an element of spirituality in your personal philosophy, it may be missing something crucial about what it means to be human. Even if you consider yourself an atheist, you surely recognize the intangible qualities of being human and the nature of the human spirit. These do not need to be esoteric concepts, so for those who wish to be completely empirical, I encourage you to give this some consideration when developing and defining a personal philosophy.

In many philosophies, religions, cultural myths, and areas of psychology, there is sometimes a reference made to the human condition in three parts: the body, mind, and spirit. This is reflected in my philosophy. I look at an individual as having three general parts or states: the physical, mental, and spiritual. Although I see consciousness as all-pervasive and the source of manifested reality, defining it into separate parts helps me make sense of the nature of reality as I experience it. In a later chapter, I will explore my ideas about the three parts of the human condition in more detail.

45

Each version of ourselves—the physical, mental, and spiritual—all have different ways of experiencing the world and cause us to experience different needs and desires. We need all three versions to complete our experience and the expression of who and what we are. This is where I reach the limits of my capacity to articulate my perception of reality. I could write more and reference philosophers such as Alfred North Whitehead or physicist and neuroscientist Christof Koch or cognitive psychologist Donald Hoffman, but I am not trying to convince you of my understanding and belief of what consciousness is. Instead, I hope I have impressed upon you how essential a belief about the nature of consciousness is to your philosophy by providing a few simple examples of how the rest of a philosophy can be built upon this.

"We are slowed down sound and light waves, a walking bundle of frequencies tuned into the cosmos. We are souls dressed up in sacred biochemical garments and our bodies are the instruments through which our souls play their music."
- Albert Einstein -

Love

The second pillar of my philosophy has to do with love. More specifically, my philosophy defines love and how it impacts life and the human condition. In this section, I challenge you to think about what love is in a broader and perhaps more practical way.

How does one begin to discuss or describe what love is? It is certainly not easy to put into words something so intangible, yet so prominent, in our lives. However, if we are going to create a philosophy that supports happiness, I am convinced that love needs to be integrated into our belief system. If we rely on modern cultural memes to inform us of what love is, we will be left with a one-dimensional and flawed understanding of the prominent role I believe it plays in our entire experience. Unfortunately, the most common way love is portrayed in pop culture, whether in literature, film, or music, is often as unauthentic as the way happiness is portrayed by advertising trying to sell you a product.

Surely each of us has a sense that we want to be loved and have love to give. We intuitively know that having love in our lives brings us happiness. For this reason, it makes sense to me to better understand what love means to us and to reflect on our current beliefs about it.

What is love?

How do we learn the meaning of words? We learn some definitions from our parents and school, but most words we learn by hearing or seeing them used in context. Sometimes people use words the same way they have seen them used and assume they know the definition. How often do you question the common use of words? Languages evolve and so does the use of our words, often through repeated misuse. I have an interest in words and how we consciously and unconsciously interpret them. As we continue, I encourage you to reconsider the meaning and use of a number of words to help you more accurately define your philosophy. In this section, I would like to examine the meaning of love.

Let's start by looking at some of our cultural references to love. In John Steinbeck's novel *East of Eden*, a character named Mr. Edwards apparently falls in love with a woman named Katherine. He describes this love as a weakness, something that distorts one's better judgement. "Love, to a man like Mr. Edwards, is a crippling emotion," writes Steinbeck. Katherine has this effect on many men and uses it to manipulate them. As much as I respect and admire Steinbeck's writing, this description of love is no more accurate in my eyes than the images conjured by most love songs or love's portrayal in romantic comedies. In pop culture, we learn that love hurts and love is blind. We are told love is something to fight and struggle for. Love can be stolen or discarded. It's no wonder that love is so confusing for so many people.

Love is not transactional. If you do this for me or act this way, then I will love you. If someone buys an expensive gift for someone they profess to love, is this love? Even if they have a great deal of affection or physical attraction and the other person responds with great affection, is this love? If we feel jealousy or the sense that we cannot live without someone, is this love? If we find someone or something beautiful or aesthetically pleasing, is this love?

The Greeks used different words for what we now only refer to as love. The desire and arousal most people feel in the early stages of a relationship was referred to as eros. A deep and intimate friendship was referred to as philia but has also been translated as the highest form of love. The word agape refers to unconditional love, and storge was defined as an instinctual or familial type of love. So the Greeks could be more precise than the way we use one word for all of the above, but still, there is something missing for me.

Perhaps it is because of the way we regularly use the word to represent our pleasure with or desire for something that it has almost become trivial. It seems that the way our cultures define love is at least in part responsible for the dysfunctional relationships so many people engage in. Of course, we also refer to the unconditional love a parent has for a child, but this is only part of the truth.

It is true that we can feel love in many different contexts and for many different reasons. The bond between parent and child is called love. The passion we feel for an activity or expression of our creativity can be called love—for example, a love of dance or art. The compassion and empathy we feel for another human being can be called love. Even a sense of satisfaction or completeness that someone may feel for themselves can be considered love. All of these examples can be true, but does this help you define and understand the concept more clearly?

The most common belief about love is that it is an emotion, one that we feel for another person or the object of our affection like a pet. It is seen as a state we are in when we feel strong emotions for another person. This is a state we can move in and out of. These definitions are part of why love is so elusive or fleeting for many people. Yes, there is an emotion called love, but there is something deeper.

When reflecting on my past relationships or observing other people "in love," there are many feelings that people confuse with love. Attraction, security, codependency, familiarity, shared experiences, lust, and similar mindsets are all examples of things that cause people to feel they are in love. However, when circumstances change, love fades. When we are driven purely by our biological urges, once these are met, that romantic love feeling and the excitement that accompanies it may begin to subside. People may then stay together out of obligation or for a sense of security. Sometimes people just stay together out of habit.

Within all of our relationships and interactions with others, we may experience a sense of love. You may consider some or all of the references I have made with regard to love as being true. Is that all there is? If it were, then it would not warrant mentioning it.

Many things may be true about love, but I am interested in shining some light on that which is often overlooked. We often recognize love in our expression or experience of it. Early on in the development of my philosophy, I started to look at love as if it were energy. I began to see it in everyday exchanges and interactions in my life, and this became a guiding principle for me. This is not a metaphysical theory, and certainly nothing in physics has identified an energy called love. For me, love is like a form of chi as in qigong or tai chi. Seeing love as a kind of energy that affects your actions, feelings, and experiences is a viewpoint you may find more complete and indeed more useful.

Is love an emotion? Naturally, love is an emotion we refer to when we feel affection, desire, or a close connection to another. There are, however, also emotions which I consider to be driven by this positive energy or love. These are emotions such as joy, compassion, and gratitude. In my philosophy, I see emotions as a byproduct or a response to what we are feeling, whereas love can in itself be a driving force. This is an alternative to the way the word is commonly used, and it may cause you to expand your definition of love.

Why is love important?

It may seem somewhat rhetorical to ask why love is important. After all, everyone needs love. Examples of this are demonstrated by Dr. Dean Ornish in his book Love and Survival. Dr. Ornish shows how love is essential for emotional, physical, and emotional health. As you begin to define love more broadly and understand how much it affects your life beyond the obvious, you may also realize how powerful its impact is on your entire life.

As I write this, it feels a little uncomfortable to discuss love this way. I wonder if this perspective will be discarded as too esoteric, especially when I describe it as energy. Rather than using the word love, I sometimes refer to it as positive energy. Even this will have some rolling their eyes. Of course, how you define love is up to you, but doing so is as important as defining happiness itself. Love impacts us on every level of our being: the spiritual/emotional, mental, and physical. In every choice we make, we can ask ourselves: Have I chosen out of love? In every action we take, we can ask: Have I acted out of love? In our relationships with others and ourselves, we can ask: Is there love?

Whether you believe love is only an emotion or state, or you believe it is something deeper that connects us all, the effect of love on your happiness is undeniable. A life without some expression of love will not be a happy life. It is important in our understanding of our relationships and in the way we see ourselves. In defining how and why it is important to you, you may define what makes you happy in many ways.

How does love impact a philosophy

When we recognize how essential love is to our happiness, our beliefs can reflect this. A philosophy that helps you act more out of love and helps you be more aware of the value of love will allow you to live a happier life. The emotions you associate with love, such as joy and compassion, will then help you overcome the many emotions that are not love.

Seeing love as energy has made it more tangible, or perhaps its impact more observable. When I cook, for example, I often say the most important ingredient is love. In every action I take or decision I make, I can ask myself if I am being driven by positive energy or love. This makes my intentions clear. This then carries over to the examination of my beliefs. When considering my beliefs about myself and others, I reflect on whether love has led me to these beliefs.

Our brains are hardwired to see danger first, so we are drawn to the bad news and the tragedy around us. This can cause us to overlook all the good. When we work to make sure love is present in our philosophy, it can help us overcome this physical and mental human condition. We can reflect here on Einstein's quote from earlier, "The most important decision we make is whether we believe we live in a friendly or hostile universe." I consider this a perfect example of deciding whether your philosophy is based on love.

I have compared the process of creating a personal philosophy to creating your own rules for life because some people feel they need rules to guide them. I consider my philosophy more analogous to processes or principles. Rules feel too rigid to me, but this is a personal preference. Again, words have their limits and only point to meaning. To help point to my meaning, I will leave you with this verse from the Tao Te Ching. If you replace Tao with the word love in the text below, it may help you understand how I perceive love.

"When the greatness of Tao is present action arises from one's own heart.
When the greatness of Tao is absent action comes from the rules of 'kindness'
and 'justice.'
If you need rules to be kind and just, if you act virtuous, this is a sure sign that
virtue is absent.
Thus we see the great hypocrisy."

Fear
What is fear?

Similar to how love is misunderstood, I believe fear is also misunderstood in many ways. Particularly where fear is concerned, I consider it important to look at it from multiple perspectives. Here, too, I find it helpful to consider the physical, mental, and emotional effects of fear, but as with love, I would like to look beyond the typical definitions to gain a broader understanding. Doing so will allow for a greater appreciation of how fear impacts all aspects of life.

Let's begin with the physical. The amygdala can be found in the limbic system of the brain. Its function is to process feelings such as fear, anger, and sadness, as well as to manage memories associated with these emotions. This allows us to anticipate similar events in the future and helps us learn how to respond to such situations as they arise. The sympathetic nervous system—part of the autonomic system—activates our fight or flight response. It is the physical response to fear or stress that causes your body to produce hormones such as cortisol and adrenalin. Through this process, some of our senses are heightened while other processes in the body slow or reduce their function. These are functions such as reproduction, digestion, and the immune system. These are all responses to fear and physically let us know when we are in a state of fear. Perhaps to a biologist, this is what fear is—a physical response to perceived danger.

From a mental perspective, fear is an emotional state for which we have many names often referring to the intensity of what we are feeling. Some situations will make us feel nervous or experience anxiety, while others could lead to terror or panic. Even our thoughts can generate ideas that lead to desperation or dread. These are all words we associate with fear, but is that all fear is? Is it simply an emotional response to our thoughts or experiences of danger? When fear initiates our fight, flight, or freeze response, it does not only impact our behaviour but can also affect our mental reactions to a given situation. We may have an emotional outburst or become quiet and withdrawn. Some might become mentally paralyzed by fear.

Based on these examples, it could be assumed that the symptoms define the phenomenon. In the ways that I have described it, it almost sounds like an involuntary physical and mental process. Certainly, the way we experience fear makes it seem that way. Unfortunately, seeing fear this way encourages many to feel they are victims or slaves to their fears. To have an empowering philosophy, I believe it is worth looking at fear from another perspective.

If love is a form of energy, could fear also be energy? At least conceptualizing it this way could have many benefits. So imagine for a moment that love is positive energy; then fear is its opposite in the form of negative energy. I do not equate positive and negative with good and bad but rather opposite polarities, like the terminals of a battery.

Much like the positive emotions associated with love, fear also has negative emotions that are a response to this negative energy. For example, a common assumption is that hate is the opposite of love. However, in my philosophy, the opposite of love is fear. Fear is the cause of hate, just as it is the source of everything not motivated by love. All negative actions and emotions can subsequently be attributed to fear. Much like the difficulty in defining love, most people struggle to identify fear as more than just a phobia or anxiety. It is more difficult to recognize if you don't realize where it is hiding since it goes by many different names. Many negative emotions dominate our society, partially because people don't recognize that they are based on fear.

These are some of the emotions that I associate with fear: anger, guilt, prejudice, insecurity, greed, hate, envy, resentment, regret, and selfishness. Let's take the first emotion of anger. When do you feel angry? It could be when you have been betrayed or taken advantage of. Maybe it is when you don't get what you want or someone has offended you. It can even be when you see injustice in the world. Does your anger invoke a fight, flight, or freeze response? Seeing fear in ourselves and others this way allows us to ask questions about what we or they are afraid of. Greed or selfishness could be a fear of not having enough. Guilt, resentment, or envy could be derived from a fear of not being good enough. In breaking down my negative responses, I am able to trace them back to a form of fear.

Why is fear important?

"Philosophy's main task is to respond to the soul's cry; to make sense of and thereby free ourselves from the hold of our griefs and fears."
- Epictetus -

Modern psychology tells us that there are two fears we are born with: the fear of loud noises and the fear of falling. These are universal to all humans, and it is easy to see the utility of these for any newborn entering this world. Even observing animals in the wild, fear seems to be an effective survival mechanism built into the biological systems of many animal species. It is from this perspective that we believe fear is helpful and important. However, when we observe both traumatized animals and people, it becomes obvious how detrimental the prolonged effects of fear can be.

When we look at our modern way of living, this once useful

mechanism to prepare for danger no longer translates to how we currently experience fear. Fear can activate the resources we need to survive danger from a heightened ability to focus to bursts of strength and a raised pain threshold. All of these things can help us in the face of real danger. When I was visiting a national park in Africa, the guide pointed out that a herd of antelope could be attacked by a lion and within ten minutes after the hunt, whether or not one of the herd was killed, the animals would go back to peacefully grazing just as before. Compare this to the way we process fear in human societies. Imagine if we encountered a lion but got away unharmed. We would likely talk about it for days, weeks, or even years after. We might become afraid that a lion lurks around every corner, or we might even have nightmares about a potential lion attack. Now replace the fear of a lion with fears from your workplace, your relationships, or some negative event you witness on the news. Our fear is not limited to short periods of actual danger. It manifests in different forms throughout our daily lives.

Fear can be an impressive motivator or a great barrier. What does fear motivate us to do, and how does it create barriers to what we want and need? Physically, fear in the form of anxiety and stress for prolonged periods, for example, causes the body to produce hormones with a frequency and quantity that is detrimental. In addition, the parasympathetic functions of the body, such as our immune response, digestion, and reproduction, become neglected when the body is in a fear state. The mental and emotional impact of stress, worry and anxiety can have equally negative implications. These are just a few negative side effects of too much fear.

Understanding the risks and benefits of fear is only one reason that it is an important concept to contemplate. Fear-based thoughts and beliefs will translate to fearful choices and actions. If we want to have a positive, supportive philosophy, recognizing where fear is affecting us is essential in determining where it is leading to negative outcomes or blocking our potential. It is not my intention to encourage people to become fearless but rather to encourage them to understand how and why fear impacts so many areas of life.

Perhaps the most important thing I have concluded about this topic is that people are not good or bad and actions are not good or evil, but we are all affected by fear. To understand fear is to understand ourselves and others more deeply and with more compassion.

How does fear affect a philosophy?

Empedocles was a pre-Socratic philosopher and poet who is said to have influenced Plato and Aristotle. Empedocles' views of the universe indicated a constant cycle of change, growth, and decline. He describes love and strife as the two contrasting eternal forces of the universe responsible for the attraction and separation of all matter. Although only fragments of his teachings still remain, this one concept very much reflects the core of my own philosophy. I have merely replaced strife with fear.

In ancient Chinese philosophy, we find references to yin and yang. It appears in the Tao Te Ching and is also a very common idea followed in Chinese culture today. It is an expression of contrasting states, which rather than being total opposites, are relative to one another. Yin and yang represent a kind of balance in the world. The concept has been associated with light and dark, masculine and feminine, and positive and negative. In this way, I also see love and fear as contrasting energies. Fear provides the contrast and resistance to the desire and intention of love.

Our ability to deal with fear is an invaluable learning tool in the evolutionary progression of the human experience. How can we recognize love without fear, health without illness, or beauty without ugliness? Contrast is necessary, and in this way, fear provides us with contrast to love. Fear also provides resistance. In the same way that one might go to the gym to develop stronger muscles, confronting our fear can make us stronger and more resilient. Perhaps this is what Nietzsche was referring to when he wrote: *"Was mich nicht umbringt macht mich stärker."* Translated: "What doesn't kill me makes me stronger."

Incorporating this perspective on fear into my philosophy has allowed me to make better choices and to have a more positive outlook on life. It is a belief that allows me to better understand myself and others. If this idea doesn't resonate with you, it is still worthwhile to define fear for yourself. Identifying the fear in your own philosophy will help you identify many of the things that hold you back in life. Fearful thoughts and beliefs often reside in the back of our mind, our unconscious, or our periphery. When we bring our fears to the surface and face them head-on, they are often not as intimidating as when we avoid facing them. Awareness allows change, and fear is one of the most important elements of your belief system to be aware of if you want to make positive changes to your philosophy.

"Only when we are no longer afraid do we begin to live…"
- Dorothy Thompson -

These two principles of love and fear were some of the first ideas that accompanied me in those early days as I began to consciously develop my belief system. I later found this principle in the writings of other philosophers, not only in the writings of Empedocles but also in the book Conversations with God by Neil Donald Walsh. I have since encountered this principle in other religious and philosophical texts, which is reassuring. However, even if I were the only one who believes this, as long as it serves me and does not harm another, nothing else matters.

Ego

What is the ego?

The word ego is the Latin word for "I." The word ego was popularised through the translation of Sigmund Freud's work. In his theory about the development of the human personality, Freud divides the psyche into three parts: The id, the ego, and the superego. In this theory, the ego is the mediator or decision-maker between the id (the instinctual, impulsive elements of the personality) and the superego, representing morality or values. Freud believed that we are born with the id, the ego develops as we grow into adults, and the superego develops in our unconscious through the influences and conditioning of the culture or society we grow up in.

Since Freud's work, there have been many interpretations of what ego means in psychology. One psychologist even told me that ego refers to the entire system that makes up our personality. Another referred to the ego as a shield from shame to protect the vulnerability of our authentic self. The average person also makes assumptions about the ego through the common use of the word, often associating it with arrogance, selfishness, or even narcissism. There are many more descriptions and presumed functions of the ego, and I will add my own in a moment.

Spiritual traditions also have varying definitions of the ego that point to an illusory self. This perspective assumes that we have a soul, spirit, or some higher, more authentic version of ourselves that can be taken over or dominated by the ego self. The spiritual path could then be seen as overcoming the ego on a path to enlightenment. If the ego is something we should try to overcome or even transcend, does it even have any use in our human experience, or does it only get in the way?

I take a systemic approach to understanding the self, which I will expand on in more detail in the next chapter. My philosophy combines my spiritual beliefs with psychological theories. This has led me to a very practical understanding of the ego.

In the simplest terms, I believe that the ego is a part of the personality that develops from our birth. I believe its function is to process fear. This gives the ego a clear and deliberate function that does not require us to judge it as good or bad. I do not believe it is something to overcome but rather something to recognize and manage in the same way that we want to control our impulses for hunger, lust, or violence. The problem arises when our ego becomes too powerful and dominates the mind. Perhaps a useful analogy would be a comparison to the immune system. It protects the body from harmful bacteria or viruses while being strengthened through exposure to such pathogens. However, our immune system can also work against us in the form of autoimmune problems such as allergies or diseases like type one diabetes, which is when the body attacks the cells that produce insulin.

As part of the act of processing our fears, we will see the ego trigger a wide variety of fear-based responses and emotions. It will develop strategies and barriers to deal with fear. In this way, I see the ego as a mental construct and a part of the system that is our personality. It helps us deal with the fears we are confronted with, ideally allowing us to avoid becoming overwhelmed and intimidated. These attributes may show themselves in the form of confidence or determination. However, if the ego grows too dominant in our personality, we will exhibit the traits we often associate with ego.

This is a brief overview of some definitions and perspectives on the ego. If this concept is important to you, I encourage you to explore it more deeply.

Why is ego important?

The journey of personal development is one of self-discovery. If you told people that you want to travel because you want to find yourself, many would find this a strange concept, whether they admit this to you or not. Logic might tell you that you are right here and you spend every moment of your life as you. What or who are you trying to find? When we recognize that we are complex beings with many aspects of our personality that can be viewed from many perspectives, it will become easier to understand ourselves and others. The ego is one of those aspects or components of what makes you, you.

If there is a distinct decision-maker integrated into your personality, wouldn't you want to understand what it is and how it works? If you are identified with your ego, in other words, if you cannot distinguish between the you who experiences the world and the thoughts or voices in your head, change will be difficult. When you recognize the ego as a mental construct or a program in your mind or an aspect of your personality, it becomes easier to observe. Through this process, you may be able to identify how your ego affects you and the strategies it uses to influence your behaviour.

Each of us is a system or rather multiple systems, and the parts that make up our personality all influence that system. I will expand on the complexities of the self and my philosophy in the next chapter. The ego is perhaps one of the easiest components to identify and the most impactful in our day-to-day lives. When you learn to manage the relationship with your ego, you will live a life less influenced by fear and more driven by love.

How does ego impact a philosophy?

"Whenever I climb I am followed by a dog called Ego"
- Friedrich Nietzsche -

If the ego affects our judgement and decision-making, it has also infiltrated our belief system. We will have adopted beliefs that are meant to protect us but are developed through a fear-based perspective. Where you find fear in your philosophy, the ego will surely have played a role.

Giving the ego a name or definition is not about finding something to blame for what we do wrong or the mistakes we perceive to have made. Passing off responsibility or using the ego as an excuse will only make it stronger. Seeing yourself as the victim of your ego is disempowering and will reinforce the ego's parental role within your personality system. For anyone who has ever been a dog owner, if your dog feels it is his job to lead the pack, you will have a problem. The dog wants to serve and play its role in the pack/family, but if it is required to lead the pack, it will be overwhelmed and develop dysfunctional behaviours, disrupting rather than supporting. The same is true of the ego. If you let your ego lead your personality, the system will become dysfunctional. This is why I like the above quote by Nietzsche. When a dog is well-trained, it can be a faithful companion.

Keeping the ego in check requires awareness, but a good strategy is also helpful. This book is not just about beliefs but also about strategies, and developing one for your ego may be one of the first strategies you want to develop. In some people, the ego may act like an insecure, overprotective parent. Getting angry at yourself or berating your ego with negative self-talk will only inflame the issue. One strategy can be to comfort and reassure your ego. This may be the best way to calm it. If the ego responds to fear, redirecting your inner dialogue to reduce fear by reframing the situation in a more positive way will be helpful. If the metaphor of the dog resonates with you, keep in mind that the best way to train a dog is through demonstrating clear rules and guidelines consistently in a firm, patient, fair, and loving manner.

I have met people who felt that having a strong, well-developed ego is important in some situations. Such people believe that to be a strong, confident leader, the frontman for a band, or the star of a sports team, the ego would provide the confidence and necessary bravado. This is an example of not only a particular definition of ego but also a set of beliefs around this definition. If this philosophy serves the person who believes in it, who am I to discourage it? The key is to have a carefully considered philosophy around ego, being clear about how it affects your life.

As you read through this book, it may help you to look for ways that fear and ego have impacted your beliefs in the various areas of life. Hopefully, the ideas I have shared about different perspectives on the ego will help prompt useful reflection.

Intuition
What is intuition?
As with the ego, psychology and spiritual philosophies have something to say about intuition. Science often refers to intuitions as the conclusions we come to from experience or our exposure to a given subject or topic. In his book, *Thinking Fast and Slow*, Daniel Kahneman, winner of the Nobel Prize in Economics, discusses intuitions as if they were reflexive notions about situations or topics. He points out that these snap judgements are often wrong and fuelled by personal biases. This is the fast thinking he refers to in the title of his book. His work is brilliant, and his research confirms his findings, but this is not how I define intuition.

In Malcolm Gladwell's book *Blink*, he explores the ability of people to know things without careful consideration. The book considers how some people are very successful in making snap decisions without thinking about them carefully, while others continue to repeat mistakes and failures with this approach. This kind of intuition seems to result from the aggregate of a person's acquired knowledge and experience rather than instant recall of specific facts at the moment. Gladwell refers to this as the ability to think without thinking. This comes closer to my definition of intuition.

In some spiritual traditions, intuition is considered a heightened ability to know and perceive things. Many such beliefs refer to a higher self and consider a higher level of consciousness as the source of intuition. Carl Jung also had a psychological model that included the collective unconscious. In his model, Jung considers this layer of our consciousness to contain the accumulated collective experiences of humanity. Perhaps this layer of consciousness could be the source of intuition.

Only the mind communicates in a way that translates ideas into language. Our unconscious mind, which may consist of many levels of consciousness, communicates in feelings. Emotion is often the way we translate these feelings. My belief is that intuition is communication from our unconscious. I believe that we are an extension of universal consciousness, and intuition can be the signal for the wisdom and understanding accumulated in the systems within our mind, as well as from high levels of consciousness, such as a higher self. I believe we have access to a source of knowledge and understanding far beyond what is stored on the internet or any computing cloud. This belief has served me well, and my experience has been such that when I ignore my intuitive inner signals, I have almost always been unhappy with the outcome.

Why is intuition important?

The mind, or human consciousness, has often been explained through the metaphor of an iceberg. What is above the surface, or what we are aware of, is only a small portion of what is happening in the mind. Although science and psychology have made immense progress in our understanding of the mind and the brain, much remains a mystery. And yet it seems that our entire experience is processed through the brain and the mind. Below the surface of our awareness, we store memories, fears, and instincts, and from below the surface come creativity, inspiration, and intuition.

Einstein claimed he did not come up with his best ideas through conscious rational thought. If he had an important decision to make or a problem he was trying to solve, he would go for a walk or play his violin. He was aware that his most powerful mental ability lies below the surface of his consciousness and beyond his rational mind.

When you have an idea, is it dictated to you? Probably not. Even when I write, the ideas flow through me, and then I go back to see how I have translated the ideas that came from my unconscious. Sometimes when I read what I have written, it seems foreign even to me. When I have an intuitive impulse, it is a feeling that arises in me from the same place my creativity and other inspirations come from.

In my philosophy, intuition also has an important relationship with fear. Some would say that fear is necessary to help us avoid danger and perhaps to keep us from doing wrong to others, the latter being the basis for our entire justice system. Fear is used as a deterrent to encourage us to follow rules and laws. If we could overcome fear, would we then all become lawless savages? Unless you are among the small fraction of the population with a psychopathic lack of empathy or emotion, I doubt it. If we can learn to tune in to our intuition, allowing it to come through despite our mental and physical distractions, we will not need fear to avoid danger. For me, intuition is love. It communicates the loving desires and needs of our higher self or deeper authentic level of consciousness that resides beyond fear.

Regardless of what you believe intuition is or how it is generated, gaining awareness and understanding of your inner guidance system is key to a happy life. We have all had a gut feeling about things we couldn't explain. To better use this ability, it is helpful to get clear on your beliefs about it.

How does intuition impact a philosophy?
Even with a well-developed and clearly defined personal philosophy, we will not know the right answers or decisions to take in every moment. The more we practise and internalize our philosophy, the more

these beliefs will help guide our impulses. These feelings that guide us are our intuition, and by creating awareness of this inner guidance within our philosophy, we can learn to trust ourselves more and make decisions based on our values.

Defining more clearly what you believe intuition is can be an important starting point for determining if and how intuition fits into your philosophy. If you don't believe in hunches or gut feelings, then this belief will guide your philosophy, but clearly, it will not be part of your foundation. If, however, you believe that our feelings can sometimes be valuable information that can help guide you regardless of their origin, it is worth exploring further.

Depending on the culture you grew up in or the family influences you had, there may be a belief in your existing philosophy that says you can't just trust your feelings. We must be rational due to the fallibility of our feelings. After all, feelings can be influenced by many factors.

The things we internalize, like our beliefs, will inevitably influence our impulses and intuitions. A strong set of beliefs about intuition will not guarantee that you will not sometimes be influenced by the fears you have internalized. This can make it difficult to know whether the impulse you are feeling is the result of your intuition, some biased belief, or an unconscious fear. This is where people often lose faith in their ability to trust their inner signals.

If you are going to develop helpful beliefs around intuition and trust those beliefs, it is helpful to learn to distinguish between intuition and fear or bias. "The quieter you become, the more you can hear," says Ram Dass. This may be true of communication with others, but it is also usually true of hearing or sensing your intuition.

I once took part in an intuition retreat, and after two days of exercises, we put our skills to work on the final test. Each of us was taken away from the base camp, blindfolded, and told to find our way back using our intuition, along with a bell that was sounded every ten minutes or so to help with orientation. Some took longer than others, but everyone found their way back without issue. Although many people use these skills naturally, many of us need to learn to use our intuition. It requires practice.

This has been a summary of the foundations of my philosophy. I have added other ideas that I have considered to add context. Most of my philosophy is built on these principles, so I will refer back to them as we continue.

At this point, I would like to repeat that sharing my foundation and some contrasting views is meant to encourage my readers to explore these topics more deeply. Like my first meditation teacher who shared a vision of God and the universe in a way that allowed me to consider spirituality from new perspectives, I hope to have the same effect on you.

Questions

Are there any beliefs that you can identify as fundamental in your life? If so,

- How do they impact the various areas of your life?
- Do these beliefs help you make choices?
- Do they help you gain clarity in your life?
- Are these beliefs relevant to most areas of your life?

4 SELF

"Who are we but the stories we tell ourselves, about ourselves, and believe?"
- Scott Turow -

The beliefs you have about yourself are almost certainly the part of your philosophy that most strongly impacts your success and happiness. Think about the beliefs you are aware of about your identity, abilities, preferences, and appearance. Now consider that most of the beliefs you have internalized are below the surface of your awareness. In the depths of your psyche below your awareness lie your beliefs, perhaps based on a loving awareness of your potential and divine nature or maybe a fear-based sense of disconnection, inadequacy, and insecurity. These are the areas I will be encouraging you to explore in this chapter.

No matter how happy their childhood or how loving their parents were, most people have some negative beliefs about themselves. As I pointed out in the Beliefs chapter, I consider three general areas that contribute to the development of our beliefs: experience, environment, and repetitive thoughts. When combined with the fact that our most impactful memories are those associated with a high level of emotion, it is easy to see how many negative beliefs can become anchored in our unconscious. This means that the experiences you have had, the environment you grew up in, and the thoughts you kept thinking about yourself will have played a significant role in creating your self-image.

So many of our negative beliefs stem from the idea that we are not good enough as we are. I was always surprised when people saw potential in me because I saw myself as flawed and inadequate for most of my life. To overcome this, I had to develop an external persona that would cover up the weak and defective person I perceived myself to be. The three labels that stuck with me from childhood and youth were: lazy, worthless, and good for nothing. Naturally, I heard many other words used to describe me, but these are the ones I internalized. Upon these three words, more beliefs developed, along with strategies for life based on these beliefs. Admittedly, these have been the most difficult beliefs to overcome, but freeing myself from such beliefs has also made the biggest impact on my life.

To help change the multitude of negative limiting beliefs you may have about yourself, we will look at ways to identify and change these into a positive, supportive philosophy. First, however, I would like to help you look at who you are on a deeper level and from different perspectives. With a better understanding of yourself, change will be easier and more productive.

The value of self

I have heard Russell Brand, comedian/entertainer turned purveyor of spiritual wisdom and engager of political discourse, talk about his desire for a loss of self. This is no doubt adopted from spiritual practices which encourage the dissolution of the self. As much as I respect and appreciate his work, in this case, I take quite a different view. Perhaps this is because I see the ego as just one component of the personality, and even then, I see it as an essential contributor to the human experience. In my philosophy, the experience of the individual self is essential to the growth of the whole, collective consciousness, and society.

From a spiritual perspective, if we are a focused extension of consciousness, a single beam of light emanating from some central source energy, why would the expressed manifestation of this be something to overcome? It is only when we become lost in or overwhelmed by certain aspects of the self that we lose the connection to the whole of what we are. I do not see the self as an obstacle to overcome but a system that requires stewardship and a sort of self-parenting. Do we want to get rid of or dissolve the family, communities, or society because of their dysfunction? We can see our inner systems reflected in our outer world through the people we have in our lives and our relationship with them. For me, this is part of our learning journey, which is the nature and purpose of the human condition.

As much as we may have many things in common, our experiences are different. Even identical twins raised in the same household do not have identical experiences. Our unique experiences create different perspectives and allow our potential to unfold. Each of us has the potential to make a contribution, even if that is not obvious to us. This is the value and purpose I see in the self. Each of our individual experiences is valuable.

In his book *The Wisdom of Crowds*, James Surowiecki points out that large groups of diverse people are more intelligent in aggregate and are often more accurate than individual experts. This, to me, points to the most important aspect of diversity. Each of our individual experiences contributes to the whole, whether it be a family, a community, or a nation. These diverse inputs support the positive evolution of our understanding and our cultures. This also reinforces the importance that each of us overcome our inner dysfunctions to help us find the purpose, inspiration, and inner peace that underlies and creates happiness.

In his book *The Seven Habits of Highly Effective People*, Stephen Covey refers to the three phases of human development. We come into the world dependent on our parents, family, and community. As we grow into adults, we may seek independence as part of our quest for self-realization. This may be what Jung referred to as the individuation process. Finally, as we mature, we recognize our interdependence.

As one of my instructors, Dr. Klaus Horn, explained during a class as part of my coaching certification, there is no getting rid of any of the parts that make up your personality. For these reasons, I encourage you to look at the self from multiple perspectives. Recognize the value in the whole of who you are while accepting, nurturing, and coming to terms with the parts that contribute to that whole. I hope to stimulate this contemplation in the sections to follow. As you begin to consider the different aspects and ways you can see yourself, you may be able to develop a philosophy of self that helps you recognize your value and supports your happiness.

Who am I?

In ancient Greek culture, those visiting the Temple of Apollo in Delphi to ask questions to the Oracle would first be instructed to investigate themselves before asking questions of the gods. For this reason, one of the maxims engraved at the entrance of the ancient temple reads: "Know thyself." This instruction seems like a tall order, and I sometimes wonder if it is even possible in its fullest sense. Perhaps this is why some consider the message at the Temple of Apollo to be a warning as much as it is an instruction.

"Who am I?" is among the most profound questions you can ask yourself. Unfortunately, as we become adults and feel obligated to know the answer or maybe become so absorbed in the persona we have created, we become satisfied with superficial and socially conditioned answers to this question. Meanwhile, others seek the answers in experiences which they think will define them. For such people, the search for themselves may be parallel to their search for meaning. We may look for this in the dreams and ambitions we have and in the relationships we engage in. So what is it that defines us? Is it the challenges we overcome or the suffering we endure? Is it our accomplishments or good deeds? Is it the knowledge we acquire and how we seek to rationally explain the world?

We define ourselves in the stories we can tell about our struggles and adventures. Does your journey through life define who you are? Are we just the accumulated memories of our past experiences? Unfortunately, our memories are fallible and selective. The stories we tell about ourselves are the same. Often the stories we tell hold us back and keep us stuck in the past. I will acknowledge that our experience moulds us for better or worse, but this is only one element of who we are.

Why is it important to dig so deeply into this question when you may already have a clearly defined identity that you are happy with? When you understand yourself on multiple levels, it will be easier to understand your needs and desires. It will allow you to go beyond your conditioning and programming to understand your inner conflicts and confusion. This is the kind of clarity that will help you find your happiness.

There are many different perspectives from which to see yourself. Learning to meditate was one of the most helpful tools in helping me explore the question of who I am. In meditation, you learn to become the observer of your thoughts. When you learn to observe yourself at this level, it becomes easier to recognize the programs and processes operating in your mind. Upon deeper reflection, it may also become more difficult to discern where who you are begins and where you end. As I get older, the "I am" that I see in the mirror seems less and less the real me. I feel younger than I look. What is more real: how I feel or how I look?

More important than the disconnect between what I see, think, or feel about myself is the ability to see such distinctions within myself. Once we become aware of this observer beyond our thoughts, perhaps the most profound question is: Who is the observer? Who is having the experience? If I can make distinctions and see separate parts of myself or experience myself on different levels, who is this seer? This is not a question to jump to conclusions about. It is a question that may accompany you for a lifetime if you are interested in better understanding yourself and your experience. To give you some things to think about on this topic, I will share a few vantage points from which I have learned to look at myself.

Levels of experience

As I explained briefly in the section on consciousness, I try to look at experience from three different perspectives, or you might say I perceive three levels of experience: the physical, mental, and spiritual. Using this model helps me to be more self-aware and gives me a better understanding of my human experience.

As children, we don't understand why we are cranky or upset, but as adults, we recognize that we may be hungry or tired. This is what it means to recognize the physical experience. We are affected by thirst and hunger, fatigue and excitement, and stress and fear. Our bodies produce hormones and neurotransmitters that affect our feelings and energy level. We experience pain and pleasure as well as urges and cravings.

To optimize the physical experience, there are different ways to see the body and your relationship to it. By simply acknowledging that you have a relationship with your body, it is an admission that something is distinct and separate from you and your physical body. So who are you? Are you a brain manoeuvring a machine called the body? But the brain is part of the body. Are you a soul or spirit inhabiting a body? Are you an extension of consciousness manifested in physical form? There are many ways you could define the body relative to your experience.

Even if we are physically focused, the mind is the part we most strongly identify with. It is where we often feel the self resides. For me, the mental is the connection point where consciousness meets experience. I feel it is more about structures and processes. As I will expand in a moment, the model I work from is that the mind is a system, much like the body is a composite of overlapping systems. The mind is essential, but over-identification with it will cause us to lose touch with deeper levels of consciousness and the communication that is intuition. Even if you believe the mind is just an emergent property of the brain—a set of complex algorithms directing our actions—if you allow your mind to overwhelm your experience, you will have dysfunction in your life.

In my philosophy, the spiritual refers to higher levels of consciousness. It is our connection to universal consciousness, which some may prefer to call God. In German, the word for spirit is *Geist*. When referring to some psychological or emotional dysfunction, one might refer to this as a *Geistig* or spiritual problem. This may be helpful for those of you who are less comfortable with references to the spiritual. However you define it in your philosophy, the human spirit is undeniable. It is the visceral element of our experience. It goes beyond the mental processes and physical urges. At this level of experience, the deeper elements of our unconscious make themselves known. This is the realm of intuition, inspiration, and deep understanding.

In life, each of us prioritizes these experiences in different ways. For many, their body and physical appearance are a high priority and a means for self-expression. Others may be more concerned with the development of the mind, focusing on the rational accumulation of knowledge and the expression of the intellect. Then there are those who focus on pursuing spiritual enlightenment through spiritual practices.

Religions, psychologists, and philosophers have also pointed to three levels of experience. There are references to body, mind, and spirit or conscious, sub-conscious, and super-conscious. The seventeenth-century philosopher Baruch Spinoza referred to substances, attributes, and modes. This is part of his "many things one nature" philosophy. To know anything, including yourself, experiencing is not everything. The ability to observe is also important; doing so requires us to step back or perhaps find separation or distance from what we are observing. Making distinctions that you find helpful will make it easier to observe.

The inner narrator

In his book *The Untethered Soul*, Michael Singer writes in great detail about the inner workings of the mind or the mental self. He refers to "the voice inside your head" and the "inner roommate." He may even refer to the inner narrator, and perhaps that is where I got the name. It has been a number of years since I read his book.

Singer is not alone in this reference. Eckhart Tolle talks about the voice in the head. When you reflect inward, the inner narrator is not to be overlooked. I have yet to meet someone who does not experience the internal dialogue that comments on many of their inner and outer experiences. Maybe you consider these inner comments as part of the inner traffic of thoughts that pass through your awareness. Our perception that we are our thoughts and the narrator is just part of our thinking process often leaves us at the mercy of our unending stream of thoughts. When we learn to see the mind as a distinct part of us, we can separate it from the rest of our experience and gain more control of our inner processes.

As with our beliefs, we often assume that our thoughts are true. We trust the inner voice. It has accompanied us for so many years. It is familiar, and because it seems to know us better than anyone on the outside, questioning it can be difficult. In many cases, the tone and language of this voice reflect the way our parents or primary caregivers spoke to us. This awareness can help you develop new beliefs about yourself that may conflict with the voice in your head. The process can take time, but integrating it into a philosophy will keep it clear and front of mind.

Once you recognize the inner narrator, the next step is to understand that it does not speak with one unified voice. In the next section, I will look at the various aspects of your inner system that may take on the voice of the inner narrator. As you read on, the following metaphor may be helpful. If you are in a meeting with a group of people and the discussion gets heated and emotional, good communication with an understanding of the needs and intentions of others can be difficult. If you step back and observe the group instead, you may find it easier to see the different perspectives, and it can make it easier to appreciate what individuals are trying to achieve. Imagining your inner voices as a group you are meeting to find common understanding may help you find clarity and meaning from your inner chatter.

The systemic self
In The Foundation chapter, I shared my beliefs and a model, which helped me make sense of many of my inner workings. I pointed out my definition of the ego and intuition and referenced the higher self. One aspect of my systemic approach to coaching involves identifying further aspects of self to better understand some of the inner processes active below our level of awareness.

Bert Hellinger was a German psychotherapist who developed a therapeutic method called Familienaufstellung. In English, this is often referred to as Family or Systemic Constellations. This method can help participants in therapy better understand the dynamics of the family system they are part of, including multiple generations. The method has evolved to find application in both coaching and various forms of therapy. The work can be applied to workplace dynamics, personal relationships, inner processes, and even to help clarify ideas and concepts affecting our inner or outer systems.

In coaching, I might apply this method to help people gain a macro or holistic view of a situation they are trying to better understand, as well as to zoom into the various parts of any such system. This process helps individuals to discern parts of a system and better understand the relationship between the different aspects of that system. This is a very brief overview of systemic principles, but I hope it will help you understand why breaking the self into parts can be beneficial.

You may have heard of such concepts as the inner child or the inner critic. These are aspects of the personality that develop in your early years. Some of them will have continued to evolve and get stronger. There is a difference between events that take place and how we perceive and experience them. Our memories of these events may also change over time. The inner child represents experience from your childhood and can be affected by events as far back as your time in the womb.

As a child, it was my perception that I was not loved by my parents. I didn't even think they liked me. Later, this developed into a belief that I was not lovable, which made relationships challenging. This was made worse by my fear of abandonment. As an adult, when confronted with difficult or uncomfortable situations such as arguments or disputes, I would become withdrawn the same way I did as a child. In terms of a fear response, this could be anywhere from a freeze to a flight, depending on the situation. For many years, even as an adult, when I interacted with my parents, the inner child would take over, and I would become the timid boy with low self-esteem that I once was.

This inner child didn't just become active with my parents or in personal relationships but also in business settings. A CEO I once worked for, who had poor leadership skills and could be quite verbally abusive, could also trigger my inner child. This was not exactly helpful in a professional environment. I have seen managers have a kind of tantrum in the workplace, and I imagined they were the kind of child that would be on the floor of a grocery store beating their fists on the ground because they didn't get what they wanted. We all have strategies for coping with fear and the emotional stresses that arise. Some of these will trigger the inner child. The inner child requires reassurance and new strategies for coping with emotional situations. As a coach, I do not work with people on these issues. Inner child work or anything related to our childhood experiences can best be resolved in therapy.

We all have an inner critic, but mine is particularly developed. It often takes the voice of one of my parents repeating the kind of things they might have said to me when they were angry. The inner critic's role is to keep you safe and avoid mistakes, but often our negative self-talk via the inner critic can be quite debilitating. In my case, my inner critic got so out of control that it would express itself aloud. When I still lived in Canada, there was a customer who had seen me while I was driving and remarked that I had been quite animated. I told him I was probably singing along to the radio, but I knew exactly what he had seen. Keep in mind, this was long before the time of hands-free phones in the car or Bluetooth earbuds. I had been yelling at myself in the rearview mirror. I was probably upset about a mistake or something I had forgotten to do. These kinds of episodes would often start with vulgar name-calling, then lecturing, and sometimes ending with threats of self-harm or even "You deserve to die." I was often deeply depressed during this period of my life, so if you experience an inner critic this severe, I urge you to seek a mental health professional, which is what I eventually did.

For most people, the inner critic is simply the self-defeating negative voice in the head that provides inner criticism not pointed at others. You can learn to change your negative self-talk, but much of this inner dialogue comes from negative beliefs about yourself. If the criticism in your head is directed at others, this is often referred to as the inner judge. This part of our personality can also be very limiting and destructive, especially in relationships. Marshall B. Rosenberg, the psychologist who developed non-violent communication, refers to an inner educator who, from his description, sounds like a combination of inner critic and inner parent.

Carl Jung is well-known as the founder of analytical psychology. His theories referred to archetypes, which he defined as patterns of behaviour or inborn tendencies. One of these was the shadow or shadow self. Jung felt we developed this part of our personality through our repressed negative emotions. As with other parts of our inner system, this is a coping mechanism but left unattended or neglected, it can express itself in negative ways, sometimes leading to actions we may regret. For me, the shadow self is part of the ego. It is the part of us that responds to fear through strategies developed over time.

This is just a short overview of some parts of the inner system that psychologists may refer to. In systemic coaching, people may take this further. People in coaching sessions sometimes refer to parts of their personality as the inner rebel or the saboteur. This process is not meant to absolve you of responsibility or find a part of you to blame. It can, however, help you understand your inner needs, processes, and strategies. Identifying different parts of your personality will help you better understand yourself and recognize the inner resources you have at your disposal. It can also help you make better sense of the thoughts and emotions that dominate your experience.

Labels

If I asked you to describe yourself, or if you were asked to introduce yourself, what would you say? You might start with your name, age, gender, and marital status. In Germany, age, education, and career status seem to be very important. What you do seems very important here. Maybe you would then share some of your preferences, likes and dislikes, and character traits. Finally, there would be your life experiences. Maybe you have survived a disease, abuse, war, or other traumatic event. If you put all this data on a list, would that be who you are? If so, what if all of those items on the list were gone? What if you lost your memory so that you were a blank slate? Would you still be you? What part of you would remain?

Throughout a lifetime, people have many labels, some chosen, some given to them. These are names and ideas that are meant to represent who we are. Some are titles we value, while others are more of a stigma. Although there are many labels people bestow on us that are out of our control, the labels we create for ourselves warrant a closer look since they provide insight into some of the values in our philosophy and motives behind our actions. They are also an interesting reflection of how we see ourselves represented to others.

From the time we are old enough to talk, we are taught to label people and things. That's a tree and that's a dog, a parent will explain to a child. Wouldn't it be more accurate to say we call that a tree or we call that a dog? Then we learn to label based on judgements: good or bad, beautiful or ugly, mean or nice. Very quickly, we learn to judge, label, and segregate. Soon we develop biases as we carry the judgements and labels we use throughout our daily experience.

Now consider the labels you have applied to yourself or accepted from others. These represent beliefs about yourself and, over time, become part of your identity. We may sometimes be convinced that we are by nature a certain way, which is, in fact, just a belief about ourselves that we adopted and then practiced. How eager some are to focus on a particular label, whether it be their wealth, social status, sexuality, profession, gender, and race. There is nothing wrong with any of these labels representing part of how you define yourself, but when one label becomes the most dominating part of your identity, you are selling yourself short.

Naturally, there are also many negative labels. Sometimes other people unfairly label us, which is out of our control. Labels only truly have power over us to the degree we believe in them. When I was travelling through India, I spent a few days in a lovely town in the beautiful province of Kerala. The owner of the hotel where I stayed was a young Indian man with a dark, southern Indian complexion and a welcoming smile. He enjoyed spending time with his guests if they permitted it. Since I really enjoy getting to know locals, I welcomed the opportunity. He had a good sense of humour, so he was fun to talk to. Unfortunately, he also drank a lot of alcohol. While we sat in the dark with the nearby lanterns providing only enough light to barely recognize each other's features, he admitted to me that he hated his skin colour. He wished more than anything that he could be white. I asked if he had suffered much racism. Not really, was his response. Sometimes from other light-skinned Indians but not in his day-to-day or from his guests. But that wasn't the reason, he explained. He just hated his skin. This one attribute and the labels associated with it made him so terribly unhappy. It still makes me sad to think about this conversation to this day.

Identity labels are only as powerful as the meaning and validity you give them. If you refuse to accept such stereotypes and let the authentic you be reflected in your thoughts and actions, you will be in a better position to love yourself, even if some people can't see past their own prejudice. Naturally, racism and other forms of prejudice should not be tolerated, but I am not sure we will see an end to these in my lifetime. As your philosophy continues to develop, perhaps you will recognize that some labels that are meant to represent you are no longer accurate. Maybe they never were. More importantly, as your philosophy evolves, hopefully, you will begin to define yourself in a way that supports and empowers you.

The observer

When you strip away all the labels and everything else you identify with, what is left? It is worth asking this question again and again because it can help you get closer to answering the question: Who am I? When we eliminate the inner dialogue, the judges, the critic and so on, what remains? Without our history, or at least in the absence of all the stories we tell about our past, have we lost something or gained something? These questions are meant to point you toward the inner observer.

Through meditative practice, I have experienced brief moments of pure experience. These are moments where I observed my thoughts without judging or identifying with them. This is a state where no words are required and no description of your experience is possible. It is a pure objective state where the present moment is accepted as it is without fear. From this perspective, it is possible to feel a sense of knowing or understanding that requires no explanations.

Perhaps this observer is what some spiritual practices refer to as the higher self, but again I come back to the lines from the Tao Te Ching: "The name that can be named is not the Name." It is a state of consciousness that is free of the personality, ego, and any other mental processes that dominate our daily experiences. From this vantage point, we can gain great clarity and freedom from our inner turmoil. This peace and clarity is something we can then anchor ourselves to as we navigate the inner and outer experiences of life.

Mindset

In her book *Mindset*, Dr. Carol Dweck discusses beliefs around growth and learning. Through her insightful work, she demonstrates how our beliefs about ourselves create a mindset which ultimately determines whether we can achieve our full potential. She focuses on two general kinds of beliefs and categorizes them in terms of growth mindset or fixed mindset. With a growth mindset, people tend to believe in the opportunity for growth and change in themselves and others. Conversely, those with a fixed mindset see an individual's abilities from a more fixed and unchangeable perspective. Dr. Dweck gives the example of people who believe that you have talent or you don't as being part of the fixed mindset, while those who believe you can excel at anything with proper practice, perseverance, and hard work as having a growth mindset.

Growing up, I had a fixed mindset and sometimes took these beliefs to extremes. This perspective created a very distorted view of the world and completely undermined my potential and happiness. One example is my belief in talent. From a young age, I was searching for my hidden talent—the one thing I was meant to do in life. My expectation was that when I discovered this talent, I would instantly be good at it, and my fear was that I didn't have any talent. This led me to quickly discard interests I wasn't instantly good at. If I did find that I had some natural ability for something, I wouldn't practise because I expected it to come naturally to me. It is not hard to imagine how this created a completely distorted self-image.

There are plenty of other examples, such as "I am not lovable," which led to relationships full of drama and insecurity. It also caused me to choose or attract partners who had their own issues, which led to codependent and dysfunctional relationships. Another example is "I am not good enough." This belief has manifested itself in different ways in my life, from not trying or giving up easily to working an excessive amount as an adult to prove my worth to myself and others. "I am lazy." This belief caused me to accept my lethargy and lack of motivation. When I was really depressed, I used to believe it was my intrinsic laziness. Instead of beliefs, I saw these as facts, unchangeable traits that defined the flawed and worthless person I was born as.

My example may sound extreme, and there are more I could list, but I think you get a sense of my mindset. Although my biggest changes came before I understood the concepts of fixed and growth mindsets, I did learn to adopt more of a growth mindset over time as I replaced negative beliefs. Had I understood the concept back then, it would have certainly made it easier to identify many of my self-defeating beliefs and the related choices and strategies.

Some of the most powerful words we will ever think or say are "I am." The statements we make that begin with "I am" or "I am not" often reflect our mindset. If a statement we make about ourselves or others is one that creates limits to future potential, it is based on a fixed mindset. On the other hand, if we refer to ourselves in ways that demonstrate we are constantly learning and growing, then we have a growth mindset. "I am working on improving." "I am still learning." "That needs more practice." These statements can replace "I am not good at that" or "I can't do that." Adapting a growth mindset takes practice, and doing so will unlock more potential than you can imagine.

What is selfishness?

Seeking personal happiness has often been seen as a selfish pursuit. I have already discussed my philosophy on this in the first chapter. In my experience, unhappy people are the most selfish people I have ever met. Selfishness is the fulfillment of goals and desires, as well as the pursuit of happiness, at the expense of others. The art of living is learning to find happiness despite whatever is happening outside of you. This is one of the most important messages that I gained from listing to interviews with His Holiness, The Dalai Lama.

Selfishness can be driven by several conditions. Fear is a strong driver of selfishness when we feel like there might not be enough or we might be at a disadvantage. Greed and envy can also come from a fear of not having enough. In such circumstances, the ego will engage and encourage us to act selfishly. Ignorance is also a contributor to selfishness. When we are unaware of the ways the pursuit of our wants and desires is negatively impacting others, this can also be very selfish. An example of this is demonstrated in consumer culture, where people do not give a second thought to where the food, clothes, or other products in stores have come from. How many think about the child labour or environmental damage that may have been involved in providing an abundance of inexpensive products to store shelves? Finally, when we are so preoccupied with our thoughts and feelings that we lose any sense of empathy or desire to understand others, this, too, leads to selfish behaviour.

Alcoholics and drug addicts can be very selfish, but they are at the mercy of their addiction and need to learn how to help themselves before considering what effects their actions have on others. The hurt or trauma many experience in childhood can lead to selfish behaviour as adults, but the past must first be healed to stop us from hurting others. Overcoming and healing from addiction, trauma, or depression is meant to lead to more moments of happiness. If we can each take steps to ensure our authentic happiness, we will be less selfish and in a better position to give to others.

Self-centred is how we often describe selfish people. These are people we assume care only about themselves. While I acknowledge such people exist, I am not sure I would consider them self-centred. If you consider what it means to be centred in self, you may realize that this is the only vantage point from which we have to live and experience the world. Where else should we be centred? Should we bend or adjust according to the external demands and wishes of the people around us?

When we observe someone acting out of kindness and wanting nothing in return, we may refer to them as selfless. This is just another example of how we use our language in a way that I find unhelpful. As I have pointed out, there is no getting rid of the self in this lifetime. The act of giving to others also does not require us to overcome or relinquish the self. Those who I know are the most giving and have the most to give are those who have done the work to find peace and happiness within themselves.

Perhaps the most important point I want to make in closing this chapter is that you are not some broken being that needs fixing. To say, "I'm only human" sometimes sells us short. The human condition is so full of potential and opportunity. This is why it is important to me to believe that each individual human experience adds value to the collective consciousness.

This chapter is intended to help you reflect on the different perspectives from which you can see and try to understand yourself. When we become overly identified with one perspective or element of ourselves, much of our potential is lost. If we let the ego, the fears of our inner child, or the inner critic become the dominant aspect of who we think we are, it will be difficult to heal our past and grow beyond the persona that dominates our experience.

Wayne Dyer once pointed out that "You are an I that is we." Each cell of your body has intelligence, but it is unlikely to be aware of the self you identify with. Perhaps the self which you and I are is to the universe what a cell in our body is to us. Regardless, when you can answer the question "Who am I?" in a way that reflects the complexity and nuance of who and what you are, you will understand yourself and the world more completely.

Questions
- Are you any closer to answering the question: who am I? Or have your answers to this question changed?
- Do you recognize inner needs and desires that drive you or that you neglect? Can you identify where they are coming from?
- Do you recognize a fixed mindset with regard to attributes about yourself that you would like to change?
- What part of your identity do you consider most important? Does

this make a positive contribution to your life, such as providing a sense of purpose?

- What does your inner narrator say about you? Or what kind of thoughts do you typically have about yourself?

5 BEHAVIOUR

"Behaviour is a mirror in which everyone displays his own image."
- Johann Wolfgang von Goethe -

The actions we take repeatedly or the way we generally conduct ourselves is what is referred to as our behaviour. The way we behave is the most common way that others judge us and how we judge ourselves. It is an expression of our personality and a reflection of our identity. Many have difficulty differentiating between a person and their actions, and we may use examples of our behaviour to confirm aspects of our identity, good or bad. One might be considered wise to judge someone on their actions, not on their words. This is only true if we want to anticipate how people will react under certain conditions, but not if we want to know someone.

Our behaviour is also a key factor in the level of success we will have in all aspects of life. This is true of our relationships and the goals we set out for ourselves. For anything you want to achieve in life, you will need the right skills and habits to achieve it. As a coach, I can say that it is most often our own patterns of behaviour that stand in the way of our success more than any other barriers we might encounter. These behaviours come from our beliefs and strategies for dealing with situations. How we treat ourselves and interact with others are behaviours rooted in beliefs that we may have developed as far back as our early childhood.

Our actions can create a feedback loop, reflecting many things back to us. We have mental models about the way the world is, but when we take action, we can test those models in real time. Our behaviour gets reactions or responses from those we interact with, and this can confirm our theories, show us when our actions may not be appropriate, or force us to step out of the narrative that is playing out in our minds. If we do not recognize the feedback on our behaviour, it can create some real challenges by possibly undermining, among other things, our relationships, opportunities, and happiness.

There are a number of reasons why we fail to recognize the feedback our external experiences are giving us. It may be that you are so externally focused, assuming everyone else is at fault. From this perspective, it becomes difficult to recognize the impact your behaviour has on others. Some people are so identified with their behaviours that they feel they cannot change or don't want to. When we become so immersed in our inner narrative—our interpretation of what is going on—we cannot make a clear and objective assessment of a situation. Neither berating yourself nor blaming others will help you develop the kinds of behaviours that will lead to the outcomes you want. In this chapter, I will try to help you make distinctions that will allow more self-awareness and accountability.

Is what you do who you are?

I had initially considered adding behaviour to the chapter on self because so many people define themselves or identify so strongly with what they do. If you ask someone who they are, many would tell you what they do for work. I am a teacher. I am an entrepreneur. I am a marine biologist. None of these designations tells us who a person is. In the last chapter, I tried to point to how challenging it can be to define who you are. Defining yourself based on the things you do is like basing your identity around your habits and biological functions. Is that all you are? Our behaviour can be a manifestation of our beliefs and strategies, but it can also simply reflect our condition in any given situation. What it does not reflect is who we are.

When I watched my brother interact with his son and daughter when they were younger, I noticed he had made the distinction between who his children were and how they behaved. When he gave feedback or disciplined them, he was very clear that he was not judging his children but judging their behaviour. They were never bad or wrong, but their behaviour sometimes was. Unfortunately, I see very few adults make this distinction when reflecting on themselves. Most people criticize themselves, not their behaviour when they feel they have made a mistake or acted foolishly. Who has not said to themselves, "I'm such an idiot" or something similar? I certainly have. However, this way of identifying with our behaviour leads to a fixed mindset because we begin to believe that our actions are part of our nature.

Many of our behaviours are strategies we have developed because we think they will get us what we want. Love, respect, community, and a sense of purpose, are all needs or desires people have in common; we just have very different ways of trying to achieve them. Some of these strategies were established at a young age and continue to affect our behaviour as adults, whether they are successful or not. Understanding which beliefs and correlated strategies have led us to form habits of behaviour is an important part of developing a new and more supportive personal philosophy.

Regardless of what others think of us or how they respond, we are not our behaviours. Our behaviours are far more a reflection of our conditioning, the habits we have internalized, and the strategies we employ to fulfill our needs. By recognizing the distinction between behaviour and the individual, we can develop a healthier relationship with others as well as with ourselves.

Is behaviour purely biological?

If you believe that consciousness is simply an emergent property of the brain, then it's possible you also believe that our behaviour is purely a product of our biology. This is a perfectly logical and empirical perspective. Does the mind also play a role in our behaviour? What role does consciousness play in our behaviour? Do we have free will? The fact that biology plays a significant role in how we behave seems obvious to me, but making it exclusively a product of biological processes leaves no room for self-directed change and improvement.

In his book *Behave*, Robert Sapolsky, professor of biology and neurology at Stanford University, details the many factors that influence human behaviour which are completely out of our control. In fact, Sapolsky explains how our behaviour can be affected by conditions experienced by past generations. If we have so little control over our behaviour, why do we judge ourselves and others based on our actions? Why, then, do we perceive our behaviour as being such a significant part of our identity? When we comment on someone's personality, we are referring to their words and actions. So if it is all biological, is liking someone for their personality any less superficial than liking them for their physical appearance?

There is a lot to be said for the recognition that our biology plays a significant role in our behaviour. Recognizing this allows us to have more empathy for others and ourselves when stress and fear cause us to act out of character. It also helps us recognize that people are not bad or evil but that we can all exhibit these qualities under certain conditions, such as war or other desperate circumstances. I also consider it very helpful to be aware of the state we are in as well as the internal and external conditions that are contributing to these mental and emotional states. However, I see no utility in believing everything is out of our control and simply a product of our biology. To me, this is like adopting a fixed mindset where we are born a certain way with certain genes and a particular biology, and there is nothing we can do to change.

Each of us can change our behaviours by practicing new habits, changing beliefs and ways of thinking, and raising our self-awareness. Awareness allows change! I have witnessed this in myself and others. Changes in my behaviour came through therapy, coaching, education, and my personal development journey. As part of this process, I became more aware of my spiritual, mental, and physical needs. My experience tells me that I created changes to my behaviour of my own volition, which leads me to believe that behaviour is more than just biology. This belief serves me and creates a sense of empowerment and responsibility.

Values

Our values are not our beliefs or ethics, although they are closely related. Our beliefs and our values strongly influence our attitudes and behaviours, while our ethics create boundaries and rules of conduct in situations that require moral judgment. All three of these influences will affect our perception and represent elements of our character.

The beliefs we internalize usually live below the surface of our awareness, whereas we tend to be more conscious of our values. Most of our values develop at a young age, and although these may not change, it may be the case that our focus and emphasis change, or we prioritize our values differently in different phases of our lives. The freedom we seek in our youth may be superseded by stability or security as we get older or start a family.

Naturally, our beliefs will influence our values, but our values are a much stronger driver of our decisions and behaviour. Sometimes our beliefs and our values can conflict. If we have fear-based beliefs that lead to negative behaviours, these will be in conflict with values such as love, honesty, authenticity, and integrity. If we live a life or do a job where many of our behaviours are not aligned with our values, this will likely lead to a great deal of unhappiness and frustration.

My values are woven into my philosophy, and as I continue to discover beliefs and take stock of their utility, I also look to make sure they align with my values. I have coached people who were unhappy in their job because some of the things they did to earn money conflicted with their values. This did not become clear to them until we did the work to identify their values. Many of us live with inner conflicts between our beliefs, our values, and the habits behind our behaviours. If you value health and fitness but are stuck in the habits of a couch potato, it is likely you don't feel very good about yourself. Creating more congruence between these areas, when possible, will lead us to more peace and greater happiness.

There are a variety of exercises you can do to get clear on your values. These include numerous online resources. Some will recommend that you identify your top five or top three core values. I benefit from identifying around ten values and prioritizing them from there. You can start by asking straightforward questions like, "What's important to me?" or "What matters to me most?" To help clarify your values, I recommend you take a blank sheet of paper and fill the page with as many values as you can think of. There are hundreds of possibilities. I don't recommend lists, but instead, write these words in random places all over the sheet of paper. These are words such as courage, family, ambition, trust, honesty, adventure, determination, and freedom. Once you have filled the page, start crossing off the ones that are unimportant to you. Think of the things you would be willing to compromise or live without. As you continue to cross off words, it will likely get harder and harder, but try to cross off all but the last ten values. What remains will be your most important values.

Once you are clear on your values, it is time to ask yourself if you live these values and how they show up in your behaviour. It may be that the life you live or the job you do makes it difficult to live some of your values. How many values do you share with those closest to you? Are there any beliefs you are aware of that conflict with your values? Asking these questions and getting clear on your values will help you understand yourself and your behaviours much better.

Changing behaviour

There are a number of ways we can go about changing behaviours when we recognize they are not in our best interest. Naturally, adopting new beliefs will help you change, and reflecting on your behaviour and the results of your actions will provide valuable feedback to help you. In this section, I would like to bring your attention to two helpful processes for changing behaviour because changing how you behave can also help you change what you believe about yourself.

The first method is a powerful therapeutic approach which requires the support of a mental health practitioner such as a therapist or counsellor. The other is a helpful method for habit change which can help you create change in your life by making tiny alternations to your behaviour.

Cognitive Behavioural Therapy (CBT) has become a helpful tool in treating such mental health issues as depression and post-traumatic stress disorder (PTSD) but is also supportive in general behaviour modification. CBT was developed by Dr. Aaron Beck, a psychiatrist and professor in the department of psychiatry at the University of Pennsylvania. He introduced this form of structured talk therapy technique which can help people find new ways to behave by changing their thought patterns. In CBT therapy sessions, a trained professional can help you to become aware of your negative thinking habits and the patterns of behaviour that are driven by such thoughts. The inner narrator that I mentioned in the last chapter will convey messages which reaffirm or convince us to pursue behaviours which in turn help to confirm the narrator's message. It becomes a self-affirming feedback loop, but this can be broken through this type of therapy.

CBT is based on the premise that the way people think and interpret events in their lives will affect how they behave and feel. If the voice in your head is telling you, "You will never make a relationship work," or "No one will ever love you," you are making assumptions and, in extreme cases, creating a catastrophe out of events that are a normal part of life. This therapy can help you to avoid jumping to conclusions and see nuance rather than black and white. Remember that repetitive thought is one of the ways we develop beliefs, so CBT is also a valuable technique for changing our beliefs.

There are plenty of great coaches who have written books and provided processes for personal change. One that I find helpful and easy to implement is the model outlined in the book *Tiny Habits* by BJ Fogg. Fogg is a social scientist and professor at Stanford University. His behavioural model can be summed up in the following formula: B=MAT. He has concluded that behaviour is a result of motivation, ability, and triggers. The implication for modifying behaviour or adopting new habits is that your success in creating change relies on your level of motivation relative to your level of ability, as well as the triggers that prompt you to initiate a behaviour. In other words, the more difficult something is to do, the more motivation you will need to do it, and your level of success will be influenced by the prompts that unconsciously trigger your desired behaviour.

When Fogg wants to integrate a new habit, he starts small with tasks that are easy to complete and therefore require low motivation to do. He then finds another behaviour with which he can coordinate this action and uses this as a trigger for his new behaviour. Fogg gives several examples of how he has applied this in his life. One of these examples that I find demonstrates the power of tiny habits very well is that Fogg wanted to improve his fitness, so he decided to start by doing two push-ups whenever he was triggered to do so. His trigger, i.e., the act he coupled with his push-ups, was going to the wash-room. Since this was an activity he already did several times a day, he would do two push-ups before going to the washroom. His push-ups soon became five, and then ten, so eventually, he was doing one hundred push-ups per day.

BJ Fogg's method of using existing behaviours to trigger new tiny habits has worked extremely well for me and for others I have recommended it to. This process also works to change thoughts and beliefs that are directly related to behaviours. I live in Germany, where bakeries are plentiful. When working from home, I had a phase where I would regularly take a short walk past my bakery and pick up something sweet. When I realized I was doing this daily, I decided this was not a good habit and decided to change. However, sometimes I would go to the bakery just to buy bread, which is when it was tempting to also buy a piece of cake or a cinnamon roll. I started practising a habit where every time I looked at sweets through the display window at the bakery, I would tell myself, "I don't need that." At first, I would consciously look at all of the delicious things I was tempted to buy and repeat this phrase in my mind as I looked at each one. Now it just happens automatically. When I am travelling or at home and I see something sweet I could add to my order, it auto-matically goes through my mind. When asked if I want dessert at a restaurant, the phrase "I don't need that" goes through my mind; I need to override it if I want to make an exception. Obviously, if I make regular exceptions, this will become the new habit.

Simple processes to change habits can work if they are small enough to initiate with low motivation or a limited amount of willpower. Clearly, this is not enough to overcome addiction or very strong cravings. When changing behaviour, it can be helpful to understand if your habit is triggered by a physical compulsion or a mental one. With addiction, whether it be smoking, food, alcohol, or harder drugs, there is a physical aspect as well as a mental one. Eating disorders have a far greater mental aspect than physical triggers or cravings. In such cases, CBT can be a very helpful change process.

As you further consider your behaviour and develop a philosophy to help assess and manage your actions, you may recognize that behavioural habits persist even after you recognize and change the beliefs which led to the initiation of a particular behaviour. Awareness allows change, but making change last requires repetition. Changing habits becomes easier when the beliefs or convictions that support a behaviour have changed. That said, long-practiced and well-established behaviour is difficult to stop doing. Replacing it with a healthier or more positive behaviour will make change easier.

I will discuss ways to change mental habits in the next chapter. Recognizing that you are not your behaviours and that your behaviours need not be permanent are big mental steps on the path to change. We all have physical, mental, and spiritual needs that trigger our behaviours. Noticing how all of these are connected will better help you understand yourself.

I want to end this chapter with some ideas from eighteenth-century German philosopher Immanuel Kant. Kant believed one should always live by maxims, which are essentially moral rules. The maxims we live by, Kant thought, should be those which can be applied universally, as if they were rules everyone should live by. He also believed that we should not treat people as a means to an end but rather see people as means in themselves. In other words, see the value in each individual rather than what they can do for you. As you develop a philosophy around your behaviour, Kant provides a good moral framework. As you get clearer on your values, it may be helpful to create maxims to ensure you are living your values. Your philosophy is, after all, your guidelines for life.

Questions

- Do you recognize which of your behaviours support your happiness and which undermine it?
- What do you think you can change, and what are you willing to change?
- Do you recognize beliefs that keep you stuck in negative behaviours?
- If you have goals for your life, what behaviours do you need to accomplish them?

6 THINKING AND FEELING

"We are what we think. All that we are arises from our thoughts.
With our thoughts we make the world.
Speak or act with a pure mind and happiness will follow you
as your shadow, unshakeable."
- The Dhammapada -

The distinction often made when referring to thoughts and feelings is that thinking is the rational or logical process for interpreting the world, while feelings or intuitions are subjective and often unreliable. Unfortunately, many of our thoughts are anything but rational and certainly not based on reliable truth or fact. Sadly, the assumption or even conditioning that our feelings are unreliable in helping us navigate or understand the world leaves many unwilling to reflect or try to understand what signals our feelings send us. Both our thoughts and feelings are important, and ignoring or underestimating either will leave us at a significant disadvantage.

In this chapter, I would like to look at both of these ways of processing our experiences with the intention to understand our inner world better while also successfully navigating our path through life. Recognizing benefits and limitations that thinking and feeling have on our perception is part of this process. Our ability to think gives us enormous advantages while also causing blockages or distortions in perception. However, a great deal happens below the level of conscious thought. Feelings can help us tap into deeper levels of consciousness, providing wisdom and understanding beyond the rational mind. This is the realm of intuition and inspiration. When fear or past trauma triggers negative emotions, it becomes more difficult to understand our feelings. With a greater understanding of these two modes of internal expression, we can learn to maximize their benefit, and in doing so, our potential for success and happiness is limitless.

What is a thought? From a physical perspective, when you are thinking, neurons in the brain release neurotransmitters—the chemicals that generate electrical signals in the surrounding neurons. Thoughts then form as this electrical activity spreads among thousands of neurons. A thought process can develop when something we experience externally creates a pattern of neurons firing, and the more we experience something or think about this experience, the stronger this pattern becomes.

The Iceberg Model is widely used to demonstrate the distinction between what is on the level of conscious awareness and what lies below the surface. Just like a real iceberg, in this model, what is above the surface—rational thoughts, facts, and anything observable—is only a fraction of what is below the surface. Beyond our conscious awareness lie our biases, habits, feelings, experiences, and all things we may not think about consciously. However, everything below the surface strongly influences what we think. Social scientist Johnathan Haidt uses a different metaphor. He refers to the mind in terms of an elephant and rider, with the rider representing the rational mind and the elephant being the unconscious, automated processes of the mind. Both of these ideas will be more helpful in the chapter on communication, but for now, I find it useful to gain perspective on the scope of what lies beyond rational thought.

From a more spiritual perspective, Eckhart Tolle considers

thoughts as objects or forms that we attract to us. He imagines a collective mind where thoughts reside, and when we resonate with particular thought forms, they will enter our consciousness. Our thoughts are not just our own but also part of a collective or universal consciousness. Tolle believes that we draw thoughts to us through what we feel and experience. In this way, thought movements such a social or political ideas do not just grow by sharing ideas through language, but also through our attraction to them by our perceptions and feelings. This is another way of seeing the connection between thoughts and feelings.

I wonder if Tolle was influenced by Plato's belief that the physical world is not the real world. Plato believed reality was a dimension of ideas or forms, and these forms were the essence of things we experience in the physical world. This conjures the picture of some quantum energy field comprising thoughts and ideas creating a foundation for this reality. The question would then become, what influence do we have over such thought forms within this energy field?

These are things to consider as we contemplate the nature of thoughts. Are thoughts generated exclusively by the brain, rising into consciousness from below the surface of awareness, i.e., from the elephant? Are thoughts something the brain translates or receives, like a television or radio broadcast? Do we attract thoughts from a universal mind? I cannot provide the answer. The question that concerns us in the book is: Which belief serves you more?

Your beliefs about the nature of consciousness will impact your beliefs around the nature of thoughts and thinking. One thing I find helpful in Eckhart Tolle's philosophy is the reminder that we are not our thoughts. You cannot know yourself through thought. You can only know yourself when you step back from the thought and become the observer of your experience. When we view ourselves only from the biological perspective and consider the mind as only the neuro-chemical processes in the brain, it can be more difficult to separate ourselves from this experience.

If we are to successfully recognize the systems within which we exist, there is great value in finding separation. Observing our thoughts and seeing that we are separate from them creates awareness that will allow us to change.

"All great achievements of science must start from intuitive knowledge. I believe in intuition and inspiration. . .at times I feel certain I am right while not knowing the reason."
- Albert Einstein -

The power of thought

Thinking is an amazing tool that allows us to use language internally, reflect on past events, consider potential future events, and bring our imagination and creativity into form. Philosophy, science, literature, and even spiritual writings all require thought. We solve problems, plan our travels, and teach others through the thinking process. The list of benefits is long, but the list of issues related to thinking isn't short either.

According to experimental psychologist and neuroscientist Ethan Kross, we spend from one-third to one-half of our waking hours not in the present. In other words, our thoughts take our attention away from our current experience. Naturally, some of this time is spent reminiscing about the past or daydreaming about the future. This can be very positive. Unfortunately, we spend far more time ruminating on the past and worrying about the future. This can lead to stress, anxiety, and a lot of distraction from all the potential benefits our rational thinking mind can provide us.

Having an inner voice, or as Ethan Kross refers to it, the ability to use language silently is clearly an asset. Even if it takes on a personality of its own, as I pointed out in Chapter 4—Self, the ability to have conversations with yourself can be a helpful way of processing experiences or preparing for future events. However, when particular voices within us become too dominant or when particular thoughts become overwhelming or "too noisy" to allow any other thoughts through, we have a problem.

We all have thoughts about our past, and the mind likes to form our memories into stories. These stories often contain facts, but the mind also likes to fill in the blanks or make adjustments to align with beliefs and assumptions. These stories will become part of our identity, so it is important to be aware of what our thoughts are evolving into. These thoughts and the stories they create can become a very dominant part of our inner thought process. When these stories are negative, they can lead to all kinds of poor choices and self-defeating behaviour. In such cases, CBT or other therapies can help correct these unhelpful thought patterns, which may have become established as beliefs.

A thought can make you smile or frown. It can cause you to panic or feel relief. It can trigger desire or reinforce your resolve. Thoughts have this power, which leads to another interesting question. Are you in control of your thoughts, or are they in control of you?

There are those who believe in what is often referred to as the law of attraction. In simplistic terms, this is a belief in the ability of our thoughts to attract particular outcomes in life, good or bad. To my knowledge, there is no proof of this process or any theory in quantum physics that suggests thoughts can turn into things. Considering the topic has been written about for hundreds if not thousands of years, I also don't believe it is a secret suppressed by the powerful. On the other hand, I have read books on the topic, such as The Secret of the Ages by Robert Collier, and listened to numerous talks on the subject by Abraham-Hicks and find the belief itself motivating and helpful. Naturally, this depends on which version of the belief one adopts and how it is applied.

If we are discerning and focused on what we think, the repetition of thoughts will become internalized in our unconscious, i.e., the elephant. As we continue through life, those things we have internalized will deliver impulses, inspiration, and intuitions. The choices and actions we take without rationally considering them may be generated by those thoughts we have embedded in our unconscious. If this process delivers the results you want, proving whether there is a universal law that allows our thoughts to create reality becomes irrelevant.

Most importantly, thinking plays a powerful role in your happiness. Thoughts and the stories they evolve into or the patterns that repeat in your brain have a tremendous impact on your mental health. For this reason alone, it is important to appreciate the power of thought.

"Very little is needed to make a happy life; it is all within yourself in your way of thinking."
- Marcus Aurelius, Meditations -

Thinking habits
Estimates around the number of thoughts the average person has per day vary greatly. I have read claims from six thousand thoughts per day to more than seventy thousand. More interesting than the quantity is the content of such thoughts. Most of us repeat the same thoughts over and over again. We complain, we criticize, we worry, and we judge. Our experiences throughout the day will trigger thoughts that we have practiced for months, years, or even decades. We then usually respond to the practiced way of thinking about a situation rather than following the course of action that reflects our most current knowledge, experience, and understanding. This is where our habitual way of thinking can really get in the way.

In his book *Breaking the Habit of Being Yourself*, Dr. Joe Dispenza presents the case that our habitual way of thinking creates physical states in the body that lead to emotional states of being. He views personality as a practiced way of being, and the way we feel is often a result of chemical reactions the body has practiced in response to how we experience the world. In other words, our external experiences and habitual thoughts about those experiences trigger a response in the body.

From a physical standpoint, the more we think certain thoughts, the stronger the connections between the neurons carrying those thoughts. Dispenza's phrase for this is, "Neurons that fire together, wire together." When I coach clients to change thinking habits, I use the following metaphor: "If you walk every day through the forest, over time, a path will form. If you begin to walk a new path, there will be resistance in the form of plants and other obstacles, but over time you will clear a new path. If you no longer walk the old path, it will become overgrown." The message here is that it takes practice to maintain a new way of thinking, and if you do not create a new path, you will habitually find yourself back on the old one. This is why the best way to change an old habit is to replace it with something else.

Behavioural and thinking habits are both very powerful. Also, the process of creating habits is very helpful. We would be unable to function if we had to think consciously about everything we do. The same is true for mental habits. We do not have to stop and reconsider everything we observe because we have mental shortcuts that have become habits. Imagine something you have learned to do without thinking, like riding a bicycle or driving a car. I no longer own a car, but I still drive on occasion. If I had to think consciously about all those things I had to remember as I was first learning to drive, it would be very strenuous and even dangerous.

Our brain has to process a lot of information. To manage this, it creates shortcuts, which are not perfect or rational but often close enough to reach a short-term goal or make a rough assessment. These shortcuts can be referred to as heuristics, and they allow the brain to quickly and efficiently make sense of our day-to-day experiences. Daniel Kahneman describes this in his book *Thinking Fast and Slow*. It is also the mechanism behind the thinking habits I am referring to. This can be a helpful process of accessing the experiences we have internalized without having to reconsider them each time. However, this is also the process that leads to our unconscious biases, which can lead to incorrect assumptions.

I have given workshops on overcoming unconscious bias. An entire codex of unconscious biases maps out the biases people typically fall victim to. I have found that helping people become aware of their biases allows them to make corrections and internalize new and more accurate ways of assessing their experiences. The same is possible with our thinking habits. It can be helpful to create an inventory of the typical repetitive thoughts you have that are not helpful. Once you have identified them, you can begin practicing new thinking habits.

One final thinking habit I want to point out is complaining. Some people will have a more optimistic outlook than others, but we all have things we complain about, whether we express them or just think them. Complaining thoughts are a habit, and we practice mental complaints about ourselves, other people, and circumstances we face. This thinking habit keeps us focused on what we don't want and the problems in our lives rather than the solutions. It causes us to overlook what we have to be grateful for and contributes to a great deal of unhappiness.

If you try not to believe certain habitual thoughts, it is unlikely to help you stop thinking those thoughts. I will share some tools for changing thinking habits later in the chapter. For now, it is enough to become aware of thoughts that you habitually think are not helpful. This could be criticisms of yourself, doubts about your potential, or judgements of others. Identifying them is the first step. One goal for this chapter will be to create a process which allows you to practice helpful and supportive thinking patterns to create optimal thinking habits.

Mental models

Through our beliefs, we create mental models to help us understand and try to predict the outcomes of events. These provide a framework for understanding, but they also lead to strategies for interacting with the world. Some people will think they are right and justified in their actions, but seen from a different perspective or mental model, someone else might judge such actions as wrong, destructive, or evil. This is why people, even experts, disagree. They may have a different mental approach to seeing, interpreting, and interacting with the world.

Mental models are a representation of the way the outside world works. They are a mental process that can influence behaviour and inform different approaches to solving problems or approaching tasks. One example would be a scientist with a purely reductionist mental model of the world. This may cause them to overlook or even ignore evidence or potential actions that conflict with their mental model. Another person might have mental models based on religious beliefs, which lead to completely different ways of seeing the world.

At a workshop that I was giving at a leadership seminar in Asia, I used the example of mental models around dogs. I am a dog lover. I have had many positive interactions with dogs, so my mental model around dogs is very positive. This informs how I interact with dogs and deal with difficult situations involving dogs. If, however, someone's only experience with dogs is aggressive guard dogs, or perhaps they have even been bitten by a dog, their mental model would be much different from mine. Upon giving this example, I observed confused faces around the room. My mental model also meant I could not imagine a life without some interaction with dogs. As it turned out, those in the group had little or no contact with dogs in their lifetime. Luckily I quickly came up with a different example. There was a German and a Japanese man in the group. I asked the German man if he pictured his hometown, how would he define a tall building? He said twelve stories. I asked the Japanese man who happened to be from Tokyo what he considered to be a tall building, and he answered one hundred stories. They had two different mental models around tall buildings.

Whether you have a limiting or unhelpful mental model around buildings isn't life-changing. How you see dogs might limit your life if it leads to fear. But what about your mental models around relationships, work, or anything important to you? How you think about the world matters. Looking at your mental models can help you understand the beliefs and assumptions behind the mental model that processes ideas and perceptions around challenges, opportunities, and how to live well.

Systems thinking

The way I coach has its foundation in systemic principles, but systemic thinking is something I apply to all areas of my life. This approach allows you to see situations more clearly, making it easier to identify issues and recognize effective solutions. Systems thinking will help you understand yourself and the world around you better. This way of seeing the world has not only helped me be more successful, but more importantly, it has helped me understand the kind of life that makes me happy. For this reason, I would like to share a brief explanation of what systems thinking is.

We live in a universe of systems. There are systems at work within your body, mind, and environment. This is the complexity of life—many dynamic systems interacting with one another. Unfortunately, most people take a very reductionist view of life and approach choices through a linear mental model of cause and effect. For example, if I am hungry, I will eat. We react to the world, taking actions with a particular outcome in mind. A systemic approach would consider many or all the factors that could be creating the sense of hunger and then consider whether eating is the right solution for your body at this time.

My first exposure to the concept of systems thinking came from reading Peter Senge's book *The Fifth Discipline* more than twenty years ago. Senge sees a system as a feedback loop. The most simple example he gives is a water faucet. You turn on a faucet and fill a glass of water. The level of the water in your glass is the feedback that tells you when to turn off the tap. This is a simple system, but as you add multiple and variable parts, a system becomes complex.

Complicated and complex are two words that are often used interchangeably, but they have quite different meanings. When something has a lot of parts, like a car engine, for example, it is complicated. You can understand the whole if you break it down into its individual parts. In cooking, a recipe can be complicated, but as long as you follow the process, you will get the result you want. In these kinds of situations, a reductionist approach works well. If I do this, that will happen. The human body is complex because there are many variable parts or even systems interacting with systems, making it difficult to predict outcomes. Human relationships are the same. People have moods, mental states, beliefs, biases, interpretations, and many other variable factors, making interacting complex. The more people involved, the more complex the system.

It may also be easy to confuse systematic and systemic, but these are quite different. Systematic refers to an ordered process that one follows, whereas a systemic approach works with principles for understanding systems. Here are some of the key principles for observing and understanding systems:

1. See the big picture. Take a holistic approach by looking at the system as a whole.
2. Make distinctions. Recognize the different parts of the system.

3. Zoom in and zoom out. Focus on a particular part of a system to understand its role as part of the whole. But also broaden your focus to observe the context or situation around this part. Change perspective by viewing a part from different perspectives.

4. Make connections. Recognize the relationship that the various parts of a system have with each other and how they may interact.

There are endless opportunities to apply these principles to how you think about the world and challenges we face. A systemic approach to understanding life will help with sense-making, problem-solving, and choice-making. Obviously, there are still many applications to linear thinking: If I touch a hot stove, I will burn my hand. However, a systemic approach can help you understand why things keep going wrong for you or why the solutions you try aren't working. It is a better way of understanding things like politics, the environment, and culture. On an individual level, it can help you better understand personal health and relationships, as well as help you see the role you play in the world. A systemic way of approaching life will make the world a better place. It will also help you better navigate your life and find greater happiness.

What are feelings?

The Enlightenment, or the Age of Reason, had many great philosophers. One of those was Rene Descartes. Descartes believed we should not trust our feelings or senses but instead rely on rational thought. He felt the only thing we could trust was our thoughts. As I have already pointed out, our thoughts can often *not* be trusted. This idea that feelings are fallible but rational thinking is not remains with us today on many levels. If you told people you were going to make an important decision based solely on a feeling, how many people would tell you to think carefully and not just trust what you feel? In this section, I explore not only what feelings are but why they are important.

Psychology and neuroscience have come a long way in understanding the mind and brain, but what role do feelings play in the human condition? We live in a world that has become technically advanced. Average intelligence seems to be increasing as education improves and becomes more widely accessible. All of this seems to be a reflection of our rational approach to addressing problems and aspiring to create progress. I marvel at human achievements and enjoy the benefits of modern technology, but I feel as though an essential element of the human condition has been overlooked, downplayed, or completely ignored.

Dr. Joe Dispenza tells us that thoughts are the language of the mind, and feelings are the language of the body. Defining feelings as language is similar to my view that feelings are communication. When we are injured or something in our body is not functioning properly, we receive signals in the form of pain or discomfort. What about the feelings that we usually refer to as emotions?

We are thinking and feeling beings, but do we focus too heavily on thinking? If feeling is uncomfortable or gets in the way, we find ways to dull these senses by any means, from pharmaceuticals or recreational drugs to activities meant to stimulate endogenous chemicals produced by the body. If feelings are communication, why would we try to tune them out?

I find it helpful to look at feelings from the physical, mental, and spiritual perspectives. The physical signals we receive from the body are often the easiest to understand. When we experience mental stress or allow our perceptions to affect the way we feel, we may be able to interpret what these signals mean. How well do you understand the signals that come in the form of intuition, inspiration, or emotional response that does not seem to directly correspond to the mind or the body? We have unconscious needs and desires, which I refer to as our spiritual needs. These feelings are the ones most often overlooked, ignored, or suppressed.

When considering what is contributing to our emotional state, it is helpful to consider which feelings are contributing to this and what their source is. Our hormones and neurotransmitters affect how we feel, and there are physical ways to influence this. A warm shower can trigger the production of serotonin, making us feel relaxed, while a cold shower can cause the release of adrenalin and endorphins, making us feel more alert and awake. Exercise, music, and food are ways we stimulate the body to produce chemicals that can lead to particular feelings.

Can you think negative thoughts and feel good? I find it unlikely unless we enjoy feeling angry or frustrated. The point to note here is that our thoughts can also affect how we feel. When negative thinking habits dominate our minds, we will often feel bad. Conversely, when we feel bad, we often reach for or attract negative thoughts.

It may not be easy to be aware that our physical state is affecting how we feel. We may not recognize that we are tired, hungry, or that our body is producing some hormone that is affecting our mood. When we are immersed in negative thoughts, it may be difficult to step back and recognize that our thoughts are behind what we are feeling. To complicate things further, when there are no obvious physical or mental sources triggering feelings, there may be past traumas or unconscious needs behind what we are feeling.

Why do we sometimes feel unhappy, even though things in our environment or in the way we are living all seem positive? It could be a deficiency of certain brain chemicals or negative thinking, but have you considered that it could be some unmet need or desire in your unconscious? The unconscious communicates in feelings, not words. If you ignore these feelings, they may get stronger. Imagine someone is trying to tell you something, but you ignore them. If the message is important, they may raise their voice or perhaps even passionately scream at you. What are your strong feelings or intuitions trying to tell you? What needs are you neglecting? Is the stress overwhelming?

Is there something from your past that needs to be resolved? Messages from the unconscious in the form of feelings require your attention, and ignoring them can take a toll on your mental health.

Do you feel bad for physical, mental, or spiritual reasons? This is something that takes practice and requires a high level of self-awareness. Integrating ideas about the source of feelings and what they are trying to tell you into your philosophy will help create more self-awareness.

Emotions

It is common for people to refer to emotions and feelings interchangeably. When we feel something in our body, it can cause an emotional response. For example, pain may cause distress, frustration, or anger, while pleasure could produce a sense of joy or satisfaction. Here we can make a distinction between the feeling and the emotion. Why would it be any different from other feelings?

American philosopher and psychologist William James was a highly original and important thinker in the late nineteenth century. In James' philosophy, we don't smile because we feel happy or cry because we feel sad. His view was that the physical action precedes the emotion. In other words, we are happy because we smile, or we experience sadness because we cry. This is not my view, but I do believe that behaviours and physical expressions trigger emotions. An example of this comes from social psychologist Dr. Amy Cuddy, who promotes power posing because of the effect it has on emotions, behaviours, and hormone levels.

The thoughts we practice often also make us feel a certain way and lead to an emotional response. As Joe Dispenza explains, we practice the emotional responses that we have to certain situations and find ourselves predictably happy or angry depending on external conditions. Our emotional response is triggered by our perception of external experiences. We will make other people or external conditions responsible for how we feel, even though it is our perceptions and thinking habits which generate the feelings we do not like.

Perhaps you have heard of a celebrity who had success, wealth, and a lifestyle many people dream of, who then committed suicide. We wonder how someone with everything going for them could not be happy. Although I was never a celebrity, I, too, had a life that people around me thought was perfect, or at least really good, and yet I was deeply unhappy. This was made worse by my feelings of shame that I had so much to be grateful for but so often felt miserable inside. These are the feelings that come from our unconscious. I see these feelings as communication from beyond the conscious thinking mind, which then triggers an emotional response. This could be the unconscious, our intuition, the higher self, or the spiritual source of who we are. What we experience is the emotion, but it is helpful to recognize the source or at least try to understand the meaning of that emotion. This can help us better come to terms with our emotions; emotional well-being is an important component of good mental health.

In my philosophy, I also consider my emotional response to the energy of love and fear. Thoughts and feelings based on love lead to emotions such as joy, gratitude, and of course, a sense of love toward others. Fear has many faces and can trigger numerous emotional responses. For one person, fear will lead to anger, while another will feel sad or panicked. As mentioned in an earlier chapter, I believe fear triggers all kinds of emotional responses, from anger and hatred to envy, jealousy, and despair.

Emotions are not always easy to understand. Sometimes they can even leave us feeling helpless and overwhelmed. Some clear beliefs around what drives your emotions and how to better manage this inner guidance system will leave you more empowered and able to navigate the complex realm of emotions.

Inner communication

To recap quickly, we have two forms of inner communication: thoughts and feelings. Our inner verbal system in the form of thoughts can be an excellent tool. It is one way to communicate with ourselves, allowing us to reflect and process experience. Feelings are also a way to communicate with ourselves, but when we ignore this communication, the emotional response we feel can be intense or even overwhelming. Strong feelings that are ignored or suppressed can be triggered by external events and lead to emotional responses or even outbursts that are completely out of proportion to the situation. We see this when someone flies into a rage or even commits violence over a comment or a joke.

In the previous chapter on the self, I referred to the inner narrator. This is simply a form of thinking. In his book *Chatter*, Dr. Ethan Kross explains that this inner voice is our ability to use language to reflect and process our experiences. He calls the negative aspects of this inner voice chatter. These would be such things as worry, rumination, or inner complaining that often occupies our minds. Again, I find it helpful to identify elements of our personality or mental and emotional states associated with the various messages the inner voice delivers to us.

In a previous chapter, I also pointed out the psychological system that is the self. Sometimes how you feel is communication from one of these elements of self. The distress or upset you feel, as well as the subsequent emotional reaction, could be coming from your inner child, for example. These are all important factors to consider as you sort out the feelings and emotions that you are experiencing.

Distraction

Have you ever seen a parent with a crying baby draw the child's attention with their favourite toy, and suddenly the child is smiling and laughing again? This may be a helpful tactic with babies and small children, but how much do we carry this into later life? Distraction can be a short-term relief from emotional distress, but is it the solution for more happiness? Whether we are having uncomfortable thoughts or negative feelings, one of the most common strategies we have for dealing with either of these is to distract ourselves. Unfortunately, distraction is often no more than temporary relief and not the best solution for dealing with negative thoughts and feelings.

If you look away from a problem, does it disappear? Our feelings are signalling a problem, whether physical, mental, or spiritual. When we feel pain in our bodies, we have the option to seek treatment or to live with the pain. Perhaps we will numb the pain through some means, but this can still be a way to ignore the pain. If we do not seek to heal and correct the cause of our pain, it will likely get worse.

What is the solution when we experience emotional pain or distress because of dysfunctional thinking habits or mental models? Sometimes our thoughts bring us solutions that feel uncomfortable because we have lived in a dysfunctional state for so long that we feel resistance to solutions. These are times when we seek to ignore the signals we get by distracting ourselves from our thoughts and feelings.

Some of our strongest feelings or emotional responses come from our spiritual or unconscious selves. When we ignore these over extended periods, it can lead not only to feeling dissatisfied or unhappy but even result in a breakdown or a crisis. When we work too much and let stress build up, it can lead to burnout. We don't see this coming because we ignore or are distracted by the signs.

What will happen if someone is trying to get your attention or tell you something, but you ignore them? They may raise their voice and eventually may scream and yell at you. The same can happen on an emotional level. You may feel uncomfortable at first and then feel more and more unhappy. Ignoring your inner signals can lead to more serious mental health issues, such as depression. Unexpected outbursts of anger or deep sadness can be the emotional responses to feelings you have been distracted from over long periods.

We all have our distractions. For some, work can become a distraction for relationship troubles or other challenges they don't want to face in their personal lives. For others, it could be alcohol or other recreational drugs. Shopping, porn, binge-watching a TV series, unhealthy eating habits, social media, and playing video games can all be distractions. The question is, what are you distracting yourself from? When you discover the answer to this and work to overcome it, your need for distraction may subside. But some habits are hard to break, so when distractions become a coping mechanism, it may only take a little emotional stress to trigger a relapse.

A little distraction is not necessarily a bad thing. Giving your mind something else to focus on can be a really healthy thing. However, when a distraction is a substitute for dealing with thoughts and feelings, it can lead to self-destructive behaviours in the form of addiction. Admittedly I am not an expert on addiction. I have engaged in behaviours which felt out of my control to change and were clearly a distraction from uncomfortable thoughts, feelings, and emotions.

For the most part, the behaviours that I used to distract myself faded as I progressed on my personal development journey. This process included a variety of therapies. A clear philosophy on how to address my thoughts and feelings also helped a great deal by making the tools at my disposal clear and close at hand. Adopting healthy practices to replace addictive and self-destructive behaviours also created the necessary change I needed

For those struggling with addiction, I don't want to make it sound like it is as simple as changing a few habits. Although I did not go through a twelve-step program, I believe this is the best solution for many people whose distractions have turned into addictions. I believe that addiction, like depression and many cases related to it, is a mental illness and requires proper treatment and support. I also believe that behind all such dysfunctional behaviours lie unhealed traumas or long-ignored spiritual needs.

"It is not the case that we are happy because we restrain our lusts;
on the contrary, we are able to restrain our lusts because we are happy."
- Spinoza -

Meditation

There are two practices which I have adopted that have given me greater control over my thoughts and a clearer understanding of my feelings. The first of these is meditation. I have had a variety of meditation teachers and practiced many types of meditation. I am not going to recommend any particular meditation practice, but I do recommend that you try a few and seek an experienced practitioner to teach you. The list of benefits of meditation is long and can have a positive effect on the physical, mental, and spiritual levels of experience.

If you believe that you cannot meditate or you are not good at meditation, you may not understand what meditation is. Some will say, "I cannot empty my mind of thoughts." It is not possible to control your thoughts. They will come no matter what you do, but you can control what you focus your attention on. Some will say, "I cannot visualize." Visualization is not required to meditate. Those who ask you to visualize in order to meditate may be trying to teach you a form of self-hypnosis, whether they realize it or not. This can be very helpful and aid you in achieving a meditative state, but it is not required to meditate.

If you can breathe, you can meditate. Buddhist monk Thích Nhất Hạnh gives some excellent advice on meditation. He recommends very simple techniques. For example, as you breathe, mentally say to yourself "in" on the in breath and "out" on the out breath. Focussing all of your attention on your breath will help put you in a meditative state. Thich Nhat Hanh points out that everything can become a meditation. Going for a walk or washing the dishes can both be meditative. In some ways, it is similar to the approach that Mihaly Csikszentmihalyi points to when discussing the flow state. In this case, Csikszentmihalyi notices what conditions are required for someone to get so immersed in a task they are doing that they lose the sense of time and all distractions. In meditation, when our attention is so strongly focussed inward that we become oblivious to the outside world, it can be referred to as a trance.

In my exploration of meditation, I have been told what meditation is and is not. People have talked about different levels of meditation and different philosophies around their practice. I have meditated in groups and on my own, chanting, visualizing, sitting, lying down, walking, eyes open or closed. There is no one right way, but for the average person who wants to experience improvements, such as reduced stress, improved sleep, relaxation, and better focus, a simple daily practice of focussed breathing is a good place to start.

I would like to share a couple of very simple meditation techniques for beginners. First, it is important to be comfortable, so if sitting cross-legged on the floor or cushion is not comfortable, lying down is also fine. If you lay down, make sure your back is straight by elevating your knees and keeping your feet flat on the floor or mattress. Keep your arms comfortably by your sides with palms facing up. Sitting on a comfortable chair with feet flat on the floor is fine too. Once you are comfortable, begin by breathing deeply—three breaths in through the nose and out through the mouth. Follow this by breathing deeply and comfortably through your nose. As you breathe, begin to count down from ten to one. You can count your breaths or count slowly with each inhalation and exhalation. Each time a thought distracts you or draws your attention, revert to ten.

Even experienced meditators like myself find it difficult to avoid a thought in ten breaths.

The important thing when meditating is not to avoid thoughts; the key is your response to the thought. Will you follow the thought down a path of further thoughts? Will you criticize yourself for getting distracted? When a thought takes hold of your attention, revert your focus to your breath. This is where your attention can be centred. One teacher provided me with a helpful metaphor for the meditative process. He explained it in terms of sitting on a train station platform. The trains are thoughts, and they will come and go. If you find yourself getting on a train, your breath will help you return to the platform.

There are no goals or objectives in meditation. If you have expectations, this will be a distraction. That said, I do seek to achieve a state of meditation. I call it the thoughtless observer state. This is the act of knowing what is happening in your body and your mind but remaining detached from them. If I have an itch, I observe it but do not react and let it subside. I observe the many thoughts that flow by and keep my distance, which is possible in an optimal state of meditation.

For those who find that their mind wanders with their eyes closed, I have another meditation practice which is very helpful. It can also be an aid if your thoughts are overpowering your focus during breathing meditation. With this method, a candle is required, which means lying down is not an option. Sitting comfortably and using the same breathing method as described above, stare into the candle flame. Try to give all of your attention to your breathing and the flame. When thoughts interrupt your focus, intensify your gaze into the flame and breathe consciously. I have used this technique while staring at the ocean as well. Breathing and staring at the motion of the sea helps put me in a meditative state in the same way that a candle flame does.

When practicing these techniques, set a timer. There are helpful apps with timers and a means to track your practice. This will help you avoid thoughts of whether you have been meditating long enough. Beginners may want to start with five minutes and then lengthen to ten or fifteen minutes as they feel comfortable. If you can find thirty minutes a day to meditate consistently, the results will be felt quickly. Alternatively, you can meditate for ten minutes multiple times per day. Regular practice is the key to good results.

If you find these practices helpful, you may want to try other techniques. In Hamburg, Germany, where I live, I sometimes meet with a group to practice Heartfulness meditation. This meditation comes from India and seeks to connect us through the energy in our hearts. It requires the same breathing mentioned above, but the attention goes to your own heart. Like other forms of more advanced meditation, this requires an experienced teacher. If you want to add visualization to your meditation, I strongly recommend becoming proficient in basic breathing meditation first.

When thoughts become overwhelming or focus feels difficult during meditation, I will sometimes repeat a mantra to help me regain focus over my thinking mind, which is a technique used in Transcendental Meditation. The mantra I use is common to Tibetan Buddhism: Om Mani Padme Hum. I find using a mantra that is not in my language gives me something to focus on without triggering a connection to related words cycling through my thoughts.

Although my intention in mentioning meditation in this book is for the practical purpose of helping you gain more control of your mind and become more in touch with your feelings, it does have other applications. Many people use meditation as a spiritual practice, which could be compared to prayer. I have had very deep and intense experiences with longer periods of meditation, which I suspect could be similar to some of the less intense psychedelic experiences some people have using a plant-based hallucinogen such as Psilocybin. I have experienced the sense that I had left my body, had conversations with people who had passed, and other dream-like states. Although these experiences broadened my mind and my sense of who I am, I now focus on maintaining a regular meditation practice for good mental health, more clarity, better focus, and lower stress.

Affirmations

I remember a character in the early 1990s on the popular American television show *Saturday Night Live*. His name was Stuart Smalley, created and performed by comedian Al Franken. In this skit, Stuart would sit in front of a mirror and say affirmations such as, "I am good enough. I am smart enough, and doggonit people like me." I found this kind of poking fun at the practices of the new age movement funny at the time. Through the writings of Louis Hay, I gained a new perspective on the use of affirmations. I now consider them one of the most powerful tools that I have used to overcome negative thinking habits and overwhelming repetitive thoughts.

The ancient Greeks knew that philosophy could not just be a set of lofty ideas. They recognized that these concepts needed to be internalized and turned into habits of thought and behaviour. To make this easier, they summarized their ideas into short, easy-to-remember statements or phrases known as maxims. Such maxims included "Practice what is just," and "Nothing in excess." Maxims were often repeated as a means to internalize such beliefs and influence thinking habits.

The Greek method of creating maxims is not so different from creating an affirmation. An affirmation is a means of internalizing ideas that may be contrary to what you currently think and believe. It is a powerful way to change thinking habits and eventually change your beliefs about a topic.

It's not hard to see how statements or messages repeated often have an influence on the human mind. We see this in advertising and propaganda. In Isabella Blagden's 1869 novel *The Crown of a Life*, there is a quote that has often been attributed to other more dubious characters of history. "If a lie is only printed often enough, it becomes a quasi-truth, and if such a truth is repeated often enough, it becomes an article of belief, a dogma, and men will die for it." The point of affirmations is to use this technique to our benefit.

Some will use general statements like "I am good enough" or "I am worthy" as a daily affirmation. My approach to affirmations is somewhat different. I first identify a negative thought or group of related thoughts that often arise in my mind. These will be thoughts that cause me stress or interfere with my ability to reach my potential. I then develop a statement that is counter to these thoughts. Whenever such thoughts arise, I then repeat my statement, my affirmation. I repeat this every time such thoughts appear in my mind, and by doing so, they become less and less over time. I have used this myself and with my coaching clients with great success.

In creating an affirmation, it is important to follow some guidelines. It is important that the statement is positive. This means using phrases like "I am not as bad as people say" or "Bad things never happen to me" won't work. Use messages that are believable to you and state them as if they were already true at the moment. This is not an exercise in lying to yourself. It is a matter of changing your negative thinking by seeing things from another perspective, one that is optimistic.

A very simple example of an affirmation is one that I have used to deal with my inner critic. I have applied this to all areas of my life, and one place where the results are instantly noticeable is when I play basketball. If I missed a shot, I may have gotten frustrated. Two in a row, and I got angry. This can completely throw me off my game. So when I notice the inner critic "yelling at me" like an angry parent, I repeat the following statement: "I need a positive voice to make a better choice." This causes the negative chatter to fade and allows me to move on in a more positive way.

I went through periods of my life where thoughts about money really stressed me. My inner voice constantly repeated thoughts such as, "Why is there never enough money?" "I can never seem to get ahead." "Why do I always have such bad luck?" "I can never make enough money." I set out to create a statement that I could believe and would be the opposite of these annoying and stressful thoughts. Having written a lot of song lyrics as a musician in my youth, I also made my statements rhyme, but this is not necessary for an affirmation to work. It just helped me remember them better. My statement went like this:

My abundance is constantly increasing.
My income grows every day.
My abundance is constantly increasing.
Today is my lucky day.

The main benefit of repeating this statement every time I had a negative thought about money was that it stopped stressing me and stopped internalizing poverty thinking. It may seem like a coincidence, but I got a raise at work three months after applying this affirmation regularly. A few months later, I got a discretionary bonus, and soon after that, I got a promotion which included another pay raise. Is there a connection to my new thinking habits? Based on this and other experiences, I see a definite correlation. What we internalize impacts our unconscious mind. Our impulses, intuitions, and body language are affected by such changes. It may be that I made less fear-based choices or carried myself with more confidence. Beyond this, I cannot explain how it works, but I am convinced that it does. Applying affirmations requires very little effort, so the cost is not high in trying it out.

The things we internalize influence our thoughts, beliefs, and behaviours. We then respond differently to circumstances and get different impulses from our unconscious. This is why I believe affirmations are so powerful. I have used them to successfully change my thinking about money, my skills and abilities, relationships, and many other things where my thoughts undermined my confidence and ability to take action. They have helped me take a more positive view of life and contributed to a philosophy that supports my happiness.

Perhaps the most important call to action in this very long chapter is to master your mind and understand your emotions. Philosophy would be nothing without rational thought or logic. These are wonderful tools for human progress, but they are not without their pitfalls. There is a quote from retired NASA astronaut Ron Garan that I like. "We are limited only by our imagination and our will to act." Unfortunately, we are also limited by thoughts and beliefs, as well as our awareness and ability to perceive the world. We are sometimes misguided by our assumptions and biases, and no matter how logical we are, there are times when we are overcome by emotion. This does not mean we should disregard our feelings but learn to better understand them. When we can acknowledge the opportunities and the limits of the mind, we will be on the road to mastery. If we also work to understand more clearly the communication we refer to as feelings, our ability to navigate this life experience will be tremendous. The ability to find harmony in both our systems of thinking and feeling is the greatest skill we can learn to experience the most happiness in life.

Questions
• What guides your life more—your thoughts or your feelings?
• Do you recognize the thinking that undermines your success and happiness?
• Have you ever considered what your feelings are trying to tell you?
• How do you typically respond to negative feelings? How do you

attempt to make yourself feel better? Do these strategies help you experience more happiness?

Journaling is a powerful tool and can be used in different ways. Carrying a notebook or finding time to journal at the end of the day is a great way to record your thoughts and feelings throughout your week. In reviewing such journal entries, it may be easier to recognize or remember which negative thoughts reoccur most often. You can then use the tools from this chapter to change those thoughts. A journal can also be a great way to revisit feelings and emotional responses away from the events that triggered them.

7 DEPRESSION

"Depression can seem worse than terminal cancer because most cancer patients feel loved
and they have hope and self-esteem."
- David D. Burns -

As a coach, I do not work with people to help them overcome depression. My insights into depression come from my experience and the resulting search to improve my life. For this reason, I have kept it separate from the last chapter, although it is very relevant to our thoughts, feelings, and emotions.

In this chapter, I will share my experience, what I have learned, and what has worked for me. Developing a positive personal philosophy has played a significant role in improving my quality of life, which is why I am willing to share such intimate details about myself. A lot of work may be needed before implementing a positive belief system and the benefits felt. In fact, I doubt it is even possible to reflect on your beliefs objectively when struggling with depression. However, when you are ready, it is your fundamental beliefs about life that will keep you on track to maintaining a happy and healthy life. This is the value I hope to add for those experiencing depression as well as those who have someone in their lives who is struggling with this condition.

I am not an alcoholic, nor am I recovering from any form of addiction, although I know depression can lead to addiction. Some of my distractions and ways of dealing with my feelings at times felt like addictions, but the behaviours stopped when my depression subsided. I make this comparison because the way I hope to support people experiencing depression is, I believe, not dissimilar to a recovered alcoholic supporting others in overcoming their addiction. Ultimately, I aspire to help people with depression the way someone like British comedian and actor Russell Brand, who is very open about his previous struggles with substance abuse, helps people who struggle with addiction. It is purely from the place of someone who understands this struggle through first-hand experience.

After a lot of therapy, starting a meditation practice, and working on my beliefs, I felt as though my depression was healed. However, I realized that falling back into old patterns of belief and behaviour will bring back the previous conditions. Seeing depression as a disease like alcoholism helps to remind me that allowing myself to fall into old habits or creating conditions that will make me vulnerable will cause it to resurface. Thankfully, there are many tools and practices that help support good mental health, and with these, the emotional lows I experienced in my late twenties and early thirties have never returned.

My experience

When I first wrote about my experience with depression more than a decade ago, I was still somewhat guarded about sharing my story. There seems to be less stigma around the condition now, so I feel more comfortable sharing more details about my journey. I am going to share details here that I have never told anyone. Not even a therapist. I feared I might end up in a *One Flew Over the Cuckoo's Nest* type of institution. People who know me now won't recognize the man I am describing in this section.

The first time I heard the term depression in connection with actual symptoms was at the end of the 1990s. I was in my apartment in Vancouver listening to an American radio station when a public service announcement asked listeners if they had been experiencing a list of feelings and emotions. "If you are experiencing some or all of these symptoms, you may be suffering from depression." My immediate reaction was, "There is a name for how I feel?"

To that point, I thought I had been suffering from a chronic case of laziness. I had gone to hypnotherapy to try to overcome what I saw as character flaws and mental defects, seeking to change these in the same way someone might try to quit smoking. Since my childhood, I had carried with me a fear of insanity, and as a young adult, I believed that people who went to psychotherapy were all mentally ill. My poor understanding of mental illness conjured images of insane asylums. For this reason, I didn't feel comfortable sharing what I was experiencing with anyone, especially not a psychiatrist or therapist. I believed I would be at risk of being institutionalized. This sounds ridiculous now as I write this, but I was poorly informed, and my self-perception was distorted.

When I finally gave in to the idea of therapy, I tried several approaches, from standard talk therapy to regression therapy. Working with a therapist, it became clear that I had been experiencing periods of depression from as early as age seven. Many of my issues seemed to stem from experiences in my childhood which led to negative beliefs, poor thinking habits, and self-destructive behavioural patterns.

Uncovering the potential emotional reasons for my depression did not lead to a quick and easy recovery. Things got worse before they got better. Facing past trauma and deep-seated fears takes time and persistence, but this is the only way I know of to create lasting change. During those periods when I felt better, I sought therapy and worked on myself. When I felt worse, I fell back into old habits and distractions. I would try therapy and feel better for a while, but certain conditions or experiences would cause me to fall back into the old version of myself. With each setback, I saw myself as a failure, which made the inner voice telling me I was worthless and beyond hope even louder.

My first thoughts of suicide came in my early teens. It became a kind of coping mechanism. I made a deal with myself that I would push through, and if things got too bad, I could end it. It created a mental habit where I would ask myself, "Is now the right time?" Sometimes the Klingon phrase from Star Trek would go through my head. "Perhaps today is a good day to die." At night I started to walk to the Granville Street Bridge in Vancouver, which was only a short walk from my apartment. Each time, I would consciously choose not to jump. I was full of conflicting thoughts and feelings, often telling myself I was a coward for not being able to go through with it. Eventually, I heard about a woman who had jumped from that very spot where I would stand. She survived but was severely disabled, which took that option off the table for me.

Shame and guilt also wore on me constantly. How could I not be grateful for all the opportunities in life that I had? How could I let people down this way? I started to think about ways my death could look like an accident, and I began looking into life insurance policies. One scenario had me tripping over a cable in my apartment with a knife in my hand so it would look like I had tripped and fallen on the knife. I would make it look like I had been preparing dinner and ran to answer the door. None of the options were plausible, and looking back, it almost seems like someone else's life.

As I entered my thirties, I hit new lows to the point that I had days I would struggle to get out of bed or leave my apartment. I had intense periods of self-loathing where I would do things to push myself, like not eating because it was a waste of food. Then I would binge on something unhealthy. I would be immersed in distractions only to panic and realize I was letting people down by not getting my work done, so people would see me rushing around like I had too much work to do. It still embarrasses me to reveal these things about my past, and I am only scratching the surface. I feel shame not for my condition but for how I dealt with it.

To my knowledge, no one around me was aware of how I was feeling. It came in waves, and I could usually step into the role people expected when needed. Being with other people helped. Work could be a distraction, so there were stretches where I worked on a lot of things but did them poorly. I wasted so much of my life trying to distract myself. Maybe because I didn't believe I could change, or maybe because it seemed easier than working on myself. It was probably a combination of both.

My breakthrough came through a sequence of events over the course of almost a year. Chronic back pain led me to try yoga for the first time. The yoga I tried ended with a meditation. The therapist I was seeing at the time recommended a meditation teacher. A woman sitting next to me on a flight from San Diego talked to me about past life regression, and the following weekend I came across a book called *Many Lives, Many Masters* by Dr. Brian Weiss. I decided to try regression therapy and made an appointment with Dr. Jonni Gray. Jonni would become my therapist and then mentor in those early years of my personal development journey.

In reflection, I'm not sure I ever really wanted to end my life. At times, I wanted to punish myself, and at other times I didn't think I could continue the way I was living. I very much identify with Eckhart Tolle's story of feeling like he couldn't live with himself any longer. His question about who is the "I" and who is the "myself" that I cannot live with was an interesting one that helped me along my journey of better understanding myself.

There are still times when I feel down, and I certainly felt depressed as my marriage was ending. These are all normal responses to life events, and I now have the tools to work through them. I have never gone back to the lows I felt in my early thirties, and I am grateful and excited to be alive. I am likely more sensitive than the average person, and there are perhaps genetics and brain chemistry that play a role in my experience of depression. My solutions came through healing my past, better understanding my unconscious needs, and, of course, developing a more positive set of beliefs.

What is depression?

A wide spectrum of conditions is referred to as depression. In psychology, it is considered a mood disorder. I'm not sure how helpful this definition is for someone experiencing the condition. It gave me the impression that it was simply a dysfunction in the brain. Fortunately, there are a lot of good mental health professionals with a variety of approaches that point us toward a possible solution or mode of healing.

Depression affects a large number of people, and numbers are growing. There are indications that it is the leading cause of disability in the world, with more than 10 per cent of Americans suffering from depression. Despite its prevalence, it still seems poorly understood. As usual, in the absence of clear facts, we create beliefs. What you believe depression is and where it comes from will naturally inform how you treat it.

There is certainly a difference between feeling depressed because of certain life circumstances and having depression. Although symptoms may not be constant, they are reoccurring and may persist for weeks at a time. Even someone who is depressed may have difficulty trying to understand what is happening to them. I thought I was just chronically lazy and believed my self-criticism, negative thinking, and sometimes self-abuse were warranted as punishment for my deficiencies.

Physically, there are observable effects of depression. The body will produce reduced levels of serotonin, norepinephrine, and dopamine. You may experience a disruption in your sleep cycle, and your body's level of cortisol and thyroid regulation may be affected. These are symptoms, but the underlying causes remain unclear to those researching biological factors.

As someone who has experienced depression over many years, I see it as a combined physical, mental, and spiritual issue. I have described some of the physical symptoms, and the mental symptoms will include excessive negative self-talk, hopeless apathetic thoughts, or anger and hatred directed at oneself. You may have trouble seeing anything positive in your life or about yourself. From a spiritual perspective, those extreme negative feelings may be a desperate call for help from your unconscious self. It can point to important needs that are not being met, trauma that requires healing, or change that is urgently needed.

If you or someone you know is experiencing symptoms of depression for more than a week, especially if there are no external conditions that could be triggering such feelings, seeing a mental health professional is essential. Talking about your feelings is an important first step toward recovery.

Treating depression

Modern medicine has done amazing things for humanity. I have benefited from antibiotics, vaccines, anesthesia, and more, even though, or probably because of this, I have never been seriously ill. Despite this, I am wary of pharmaceuticals as the singular solution for those experiencing depression. Of course, I am not a doctor and cannot give medical advice. I have also not been treated with any pharmaceuticals in my past experiences with depression. I have, however, had tremendous success in improving my own mental health without pharmaceutical intervention.

In his book *Cracked*, Dr. James Davies highlights the unscientific way the defining and diagnosis of mental illnesses has been massively expanded. Davies refers to the DSM-III (*The Diagnostic and Statistical Manual of Mental Disorders*), published in 1980 and expanded in the decades that followed. Along with the naming and defining of new disorders has come a massive increase in wide-ranging drugs to treat them. It is worth considering that where there are strong financial incentives, there will be bias, motivated reasoning, and sometimes even corruption. This does not mean there are no good medications to aid and comfort those suffering from depression by reducing symptoms. However, not all possible treatments have the marketing budgets or funding for clinical research that pharmaceuticals do.

My treatment of depression came in the way of therapy, new habits, and mental tools to maintain better mental health. I healed past trauma, faced many fears, and changed those elements of my lifestyle that did not support my mental health. I worked to overcome the behaviours, distractions, and perhaps even addictions that were a temporary relief but always led me back to those dark emotional lows I was trying to escape. I chose not to pursue a pharmaceutical treatment because I felt the best way to overcome depression was to face the source of my feelings. I did not see the benefit in numbing them temporarily.

Our bodies are complex systems, so I like to consider healing using systemic principles. If we only look at the neurochemical state of the brain to treat depression, which may be the cause or only a symptom, we are taking a cause-and-effect approach, not a systemic one. Taking a pain reliever while still rehabilitating your body for the cause of the pain can assist in healing. The same goes for treating depression. If the emotional pain is overwhelming, reducing this may help better treat the cause. But suppressing what you feel is not the solution in itself, as far as I am concerned. Feelings are communication, and if we do not take the time to understand what they are telling us, our condition will be chronic.

However you choose to treat depression, the main thing is that you are getting the help you need. Along the path to recovery, I hope you remember that feelings are communication, and emotions are important feedback pointing to what is being triggered within us. If you impair your ability to feel, you may be undermining your ability to experience happiness.

Contributing factors and solutions to consider

I continue to be interested in the research and treatments for depression. The most current research indicates that low serotonin levels are not the cause of depression, as has been assumed for decades. When I wrote about my experience with depression more than ten years ago, I commented that I did not feel that depression was simply a chemical imbalance. This was an intuitive conclusion that now seems to have been confirmed.

It turns out that there are many factors that contribute to depression. Everyday habits related to such things as hydration, nutrition, and gut health have been linked to depression as well as sleep apnea, lack of sunlight, and insufficient contact with nature. Although I assumed that my experience with depression came from the mental and spiritual levels, I have since recognized that many physical conditions may have contributed to making me feel even worse.

If you think about it, we all experience mood changes when we are hungry, feel stressed, or haven't had enough sleep. It should then be no surprise that the food we eat, extended exposure to stressful or traumatic experiences, and poor sleep could also contribute to depression. In recent years, understanding the role our gut microbiome plays has increased tremendously. This has helped science understand its impact not only on our physical health but also our mental well-being. In this case, the gut microbiome refers to a part of the large intestines, which is home to a large population of bacteria, viruses, fungi, and other microorganisms necessary for good health. Since what we eat and drink affects the microbiome, and the microbiome influences our emotional state, nutrition can be an important contributing factor to depression.

Food is not the only thing that affects depression. I was very surprised to read that dehydration can contribute to depression. Most of us do not drink enough water but instead drink coffee, alcohol, and sugar-filled drinks, all of which contribute to dehydration. Some foods will do the same. High protein diets, high salt content, highly processed foods, and even asparagus, parsley, or soya sauce all contribute toward dehydrating the body.

What we consume with our minds can also impact depression. Surrounding ourselves with frequent negative input to our brain can contribute to depression. Excessive consumption of news, which is generally negative and often sensationalized, can lead to a sense of hopelessness and apathy. Toxic relationships and other stressful environments can make us feel depressed, as well as regularly stimulating the production of cortisol. An overproduction of cortisol can affect depression by disrupting the production of neurotransmitters such as serotonin and dopamine.

This is only a quick overview of some of the physical and environmental conditions that can contribute to depression. For some, improving in several of these areas may cause depression to subside. Since many of them are simply changes in lifestyle, it seems logical to try to check all those boxes in addition to whatever else you are doing if you suffer from depression.

As I have already mentioned, I have been able to consistently bring myself back into a healthy range of emotions without the use of pharmaceuticals. What worked for me won't work for everyone, but these are important areas to look at. The most important step I took was seeing a qualified therapist and exploring various types of therapy. Second, I changed my beliefs and thinking habits, which is the focus of this book. I also adopted healthier habits of meditation, nutrition, and exercise. Before leaving Canada, I was involved in a family business. Since many of my issues stemmed from my child-hood, changing where I worked and lived also seemed to help in my recovery.

For me, there was also a spiritual element that helped. I did not join a church or find God in the traditional sense. However, I did adopt beliefs about the universe, my place in it, and the nature of re-ality which helped create a new sense of meaning and purpose in my life.

There are plenty of alternative treatments that one can consider or try out. They generally do not lead to negative side effects. A study done in Leipzig, Germany, showed that in neighbourhoods where streets were lined with trees, antidepressant prescriptions were signif-icantly reduced compared to neighbourhoods without trees or parks. There seems to be a correlation between our connection to nature and our emotional state. Therefore, time in nature could help to re-duce symptoms of depression.

I read about a doctor who treated a patient with severe depression by having her take swims in an ice-cold lake. World record holder Wim Hof has popularized a method of breathing, stretching, and cold baths or showers, which, in addition to improving health, seems to have a positive effect on mood. Part of Hof's desire to share his methods with the world stems from the loss of his wife Olaya, whose depression led to suicide. Wim's methods have also been studied and shown that what he practices and teaches can work for anyone, not just extreme athletes.

Naturally, all of these alternatives to taking a pill to treat depres-sion require work. It's not easy to gather the strength and motivation to help yourself when feeling depressed. I know this firsthand. Looking at trauma and addressing your deepest fears can be very intimidating but also liberating. If you do not do what American speaker and author Byron Katie refers to as "the work," which focus-es on questioning negative thoughts and beliefs, you may forever be captured by the prison of your mind. This is what recovering from depression felt like to me: freedom.

Considering where I have come from, the fact that I have written a book about happiness is a testament to the change possible when we raise our awareness and do the work to release old negative beliefs and create new ones. Perhaps it is the immense contrast that I have experienced that has allowed me this perspective. For this reason, I am grateful for all my experiences and the journey that has brought me here.

8 CHOICES

"You and I are essentially infinite choice-makers. In every moment of our existence, we are in that field of all possibilities where we have access to an infinity of choices."
- Deepak Chopra -

All of our power lies within our choices. This is where we can have the greatest impact on our lives and the lives of others. It is also through our choices that we have the most control over our happiness. These are choices in action or inaction, but also in what we think, believe, and give our attention to. The act of creating a personal philosophy is filled with choices, and consciously choosing what to believe is one of the most impactful decisions we can make.

Perhaps we feel powerless at times because we do not recognize the full scope of choices available. Such limitations are self-imposed by the beliefs we have adopted. Many things in life are a choice. Even whether or not to be happy can be a choice.

Choosing is a creative act. In fact, if I could sum up my philosophy of the meaning of life, I would do it this way. Life is a process of creation in which we are the creators. We create through the many choices we make. It is, therefore, a circle of creating → experiencing → learning/growing → then creating some more. To me, this is how life unfolds, and that is why choices and our awareness of them are of such great importance.

I like to use this metaphor to paint a mental picture for people. If you were to equate our journey through life with a ride on horseback, your choices would be whatever you do with the reins. You can ride in circles or gallop recklessly into the unknown. You can let go of the reins altogether and let yourself be dragged through the mud with one foot still in the stirrup, or hand the reins to someone else and be led around, all the while complaining about your situation. There is also the option to pull way back on the reins, afraid of every step, or trample carelessly through other people's gardens. You may want to consider looking for a destination that suits you and ride there at the pace you can handle, sometimes jumping obstacles, but hopefully not leaving too much manure for others to step in.

It is important to clarify that I do not believe life is a process of trial and error. We live in a complex world that is not easily understood through linear thinking, reductionism, or basic analysis. A good understanding of life and the effects of our choices requires a systemic approach where the integration or synthesis of new knowledge gained through experience is added to what we already know. We will be better served if we approach life with curiosity and see choices as experiments rather than a process of trial and error.

The simple solution to living a happy life is to stop making choices that make you unhappy. If only it were that easy. With the right level of awareness and a supportive philosophy, your chances are greatly improved. The secret to living a happy, fulfilling, and purposeful life is not a secret at all. Spiritual and philosophical teachings have pointed to the ways of living that can fulfill all of these things, but they often conflict with the cultural norms and expectations we are immersed in. If we are to make choices that lead us to more moments of happiness, it takes a higher level of awareness than many, who have inherited or adopted fear-based beliefs, have at their disposal.

Even how you see the world is a choice. Take the example of Einstein's profound question: Do we live in a friendly or hostile universe? By choosing to see the universe as friendly or hostile, each of us chooses how to see and experience our world and the life we live. When you recognize that you can choose how to see things, you will also recognize that in many ways, happiness is a choice.

What kinds of recommendations are we given on how to choose well? We are told we must make sacrifices, compromises, and difficult decisions. We are instructed to be logical, practical, or strategic. Some tell us to follow our heart, and some tell us to follow our head, but what should guide our choices? Have the goals and aspirations recommended to us by our culture increased the level of happiness in our society? It is my experience that a philosophy guided by love rather than fear will help us each make choices that are both considerate of others and lead to our own greatest happiness.

Be miserable. Or motivate yourself. Whatever has to be done,
it's always your choice
- Wayne Dyer -

Free Will
You can choose a ready guide
In some celestial voice
If you choose not to decide
You still have made a choice
You can choose from phantom fears
And kindness that can kill
I will choose a path that's clear
I will choose free will.
- Neil Peart, Rush -

Do we have free will? It is an age-old question, but what would it mean not to have free will? Are our lives predetermined? Do we live in a completely random universe where it is our biology and not our mind that determines our actions? I have considered these questions quite deeply for years, and although the science is compelling, there is one question that I always come back to. Does it serve me to believe that we have no free will?

Philosopher and neuroscientist Sam Harris seemed like a good person to start with to try to make sense of these ideas. If I have understood him correctly, he feels that free will is an illusion and that we cannot control what we do or know why we do it. Harris points to the fact that the neurophysiology of the brain is such that even when we claim to know the motivation behind some of our actions, we are simply rationalizing processes that were initiated before any intentions entered our minds.

Robert Sapolsky is a Professor of Biology and Neurology at the University of Stanford. He also specializes in neuroendocrinology, which involves studying the interaction between the nervous and endocrine systems. For those like me, who don't know what the endocrine system is or does, it is a series of feedback loops which uses chemical messengers most of us would know called hormones. In his book *Behave*, Sapolsky uses his understanding of these processes to explain how none of our behaviours are our choice. The book is fascinating, and from a purely biological perspective, I can see why this would be an obvious conclusion. From a philosophical perspective, however, I see no utility in the belief that there is no free will. My entire sense of meaning in life is based on my ability to choose.

Reducing our entire existence to the biological functions of the brain and body makes it difficult to argue for free will. However, even if these hormones and neurotransmitters are the precursors to our thoughts and feelings, I am not sure science fully understands what triggers these chemical processes into action in the first place. How can we then be certain at what level of consciousness or biological function our decisions take place?

The question of free will brings us back to the nature of consciousness: in the brain or beyond it? Is there a higher self, a soul, or a collective consciousness where decisions are made beyond our awareness but still made by us? Again, I find more benefit in looking for an answer that can be applied to daily life rather than one that seems imperially correct.

As much as Spinoza, a seventh-century philosopher I refer to often, believed everything is affected by something else and, therefore, every action is a response to an effect, he still believed that we are free. He seems to say that our process of experience increases our understanding of our existence, but if we rely solely on feelings and effects, we are in a state of slavery.

Donald Hoffman, Professor of Cognitive Sciences at the University of California, Irvine, proposes the following: "*Perhaps the universe itself is a massive social network of conscious agents that experience, decide, and act.*" Are we making decisions at different levels of consciousness? How much of this is done within our awareness? How would a belief that there is no free will help guide you through this life?

It is my belief that with elevated awareness, we increase our ability to choose or allow some degree of free will. This is the difference between reacting to and consciously interacting with the world.

My philosophy around choices requires a belief in some level of free will. Without the ability to choose freely, how do we learn and grow? It is also our preferences which create the unique experience that we each have in this life. I do, however, acknowledge that we have unconscious processes that influence or even dictate what we will choose. If we have internalized certain behaviours, these habits will replace any choice-making processes, but such habits may still have begun with a choice.

Could it be that your level of free will is directly correlated to your level of awareness? This is to say, the greater your awareness, the greater your level of free will. This is what I believe, and it has helped me feel more in control of the level of success and happiness in my life.

"Excellence is never an accident. It is always the result of high intention, sincere effort, and intelligent execution; it represents the wise choice of many alternatives—choice, not chance, determines your destiny."
- Aristotle -

Control

*"Grant me the serenity to accept the things I cannot change,
courage to change the things I can, and wisdom to know the difference."*
- Reinhold Niebuhr -

One way to determine what we can choose is by recognizing what is in our control to change. Our choices give us the opportunity to take control of our lives and make changes that will lead to greater happiness, yet many feel helpless and frustrated by their circumstances. Perhaps then, the first step is recognizing what you can change and what you cannot. This is just another part of the process of becoming more self-aware.

For a long time, it seemed to me that I wasn't in control of where I was going. I saw many of my thoughts and actions in a critical light and considered myself a weak person. Therefore, I concluded that for me to improve and change, I had to start taking control of all my thoughts and feelings. My perception was of an intense struggle to overcome a whole range of inner flaws, weaknesses, and negative tendencies. I really believed that my life was a struggle with myself. Fortunately, the work that I did to become more self-aware helped me see that I was swimming upstream. *"What we resist, persists."* Jung. I learned to address my needs and fears rather than using discipline and control to get what I want.

What I mean by taking control of your life could easily be misunderstood. I am not talking about control in terms of restraint but rather personal empowerment. I am also not talking about controlling the outside world. People seeking power are usually driven by fear, which they hope to overcome by controlling as much as they can of the outside world. It is the personal power to live your life motivated by your own positive intentions rather than falling victim to the many faces of fear and ego. I refer to a process of seeing and understanding that allows us to accept what we want, let go of what we don't, and ultimately steer ourselves consciously down the road of life.

Restraint sounds to me almost like repression or a denial of our desires. To me, control is a matter of making the choices available to us. When thoughts arise, we can choose what to focus on, but if we repress our thoughts and feelings, they will continue to haunt us. We give up control by not recognizing our power and true potential.

"Control is such a delicate thing to balance, for one needs to take care not to over-control nor under-control with oneself or one's life."
- Dr. Jonni Grey -

Ancient Stoic philosopher Epictetus' approach to life was to define everything into what we have control of and what we do not. In his view, we do not control the outside world. That is, we cannot control external conditions such as the weather, politics, or economy. Although we may have influence over some things, we still cannot control other people or even our own bodies. Epictetus proposed that the only thing we have control over is what we believe.

We all have the opportunity to choose, but we often forfeit our choices to distractions, negative impulses, and conditioning. Clear choices depend on recognizing what is driving our decisions. Choosing without fear is one aspect. Recognizing when our choices are driven by biological or mental programs is another. Learning to make choices free of fear and beyond our urges and habits takes awareness and practice. Is your life simply a reaction to inner and outer stimuli, or are you guided by something more?

Growth

When we make conscious decisions and experience the results, our choices can provide us with mental and emotional growth. We learn through experience but also through our interaction with the people and world around us. In my philosophy, this kind of growth is the purpose of life. If we are an extension of universal consciousness, then experience and the growth it provides seem like the logical reason for being. If consciousness is just a property of the brain, my belief that growth through experience is the purpose of life still has greater utility than a belief in scarcity and survival of the fittest.

Our ability to manipulate our world through technology has grown exponentially in the past century, but what has happened to our spiritual development? Has our ability to engage in meaningful relationships improved? Have we learned to bring more harmony between our physical, mental, and emotional aspects of being into balance? Have we learned to process our fears more productively? If we look at some indigenous cultures that focus less on possession or power and more on community, it may even be that we have regressed or devolved spiritually. What is the best measure of this? The choices we make.

If we can embrace a philosophy that the meaning of life is mental and emotional growth, maybe we can begin to distance ourselves from the fear-based need for external growth, whether it be wealth, attractive partners, or power over others. If we can follow Nietzsche's mantra of *amor fati*, which translates to a love of fate, and embrace this life we are given, we may see new opportunities for how to live well.

Adopting a philosophy that each of our choices is an opportunity for growth can be powerful. It can allow us to consider our choices and the resulting actions more carefully. It enables us to reflect and, in doing so, begin to understand our true potential. The alternative may be doing the same things over and over and expecting different results, a quote often incorrectly attributed to Einstein.

In company workshops I facilitate, there will often be discussions around a culture that allows or even encourages mistakes. Some will say that if you are not failing, you are not pushing the boundaries of your potential. How do you define a mistake or a failure? What is a mistake other than a choice that leads to an outcome you are not happy with?

We say mistakes are opportunities for learning as long as we recognize and admit the choices that led to these outcomes. If we can learn to see mistakes as a natural part of the learning process, it will help eliminate some of the fear connected to failure. If we continue to make the same errors in judgement again and again, we may not be choosing consciously, and it is time to take a closer look at our habits and the unconscious drivers of our actions.

The power of one

It is easy to feel insignificant when considering yourself only one of eight billion people on the planet. You will feel even more humbled when you reflect on your place in this immense universe on a "pale blue dot." And yet you belong to the most powerful group in the world. You, like every one of us with the means to exchange money for goods and services, are consumers. Consumer demand drives our global marketplace in many ways. This is only one example to help you see that your individual choices have more power than you may believe.

A properly functioning democracy relies on the choices of many individuals. The culture of a society or community is shaped by the many choices the individuals within it make. With this power comes responsibility. If more people recognize the power of their choices, they will try to become more aware of their choices and their effects. Recognizing and acknowledging this power, as well as taking responsibility for it, is perhaps the most significant contribution you can make to the world.

In a previous chapter, I pointed out the principles of systems thinking. A systemic approach is perhaps most important when considering the impact our individual choices have on the world. We may not be able to change the world as individuals, but we can make a contribution. Our actions can also have a ripple effect, like a stone thrown in the water. How each of us interacts with the world has an effect, whether we recognize it or not. To say I am only one person or I am only human significantly underestimates who and what we are, as well as the potential in each of us.

"It has been said that astronomy is a humbling and character-building experience. There is perhaps no better demonstration of the folly of human conceits than this distant image of our tiny world. To me, it underscores our responsibility to deal more kindly with one another, and to preserve and cherish the pale blue dot, the only home we've ever known."
- Carl Sagan, Pale Blue Dot, 1994 -

"It is our choices, Harry, that show what we truly are, far more than our abilities."
- J.K. Rowling, Harry Potter and the Chamber of Secrets -

The victim trap
We have all felt like a victim at some point in life. Certainly, some have much more challenging conditions in life than others, but each of us has, at some point in life, through no fault of our own, experi-

enced some form of struggle or misfortune. Being a victim is a role that you can play, and doing so leads to beliefs about who you are and what you are capable of. I call it a trap because it gives us comfort while confining us to an identity that will not support our happiness or our potential for growth.

I've spent a lot of time feeling like a victim, but not for reasons you might think. I have felt like a victim of circumstances, a victim of an unfair system, but most of all, I have felt like a victim of being born into a flawed and deficient body and mind. While therapists were telling me I was a victim of abuse, I saw myself as a victim of being born lazy, talentless, worthless, and a little insane. Why couldn't I have been born more like someone else? This is the statement of a self-identifying victim. It was a question I often asked in my youth and my twenties.

I have seen people who have suffered injustice and hardship. Relative to them, I cannot call myself a victim. Such people have taught me a great deal. People who are poor and still feel grateful for what they have. People with disabilities who focus on their strengths. People who have been abused or discriminated against and find the strength to forgive and find empathy for those who have wronged them. None of these people see themselves as victims, and that is their strength.

No matter how good your life is or how many opportunities lay before you, it is easy to fall into the victim trap. After years of practicing beliefs that did not allow me to see myself as a victim, I caught myself doing just that. When my marriage ended and people asked me what happened, I thought I was telling an accurate account of what went wrong. I was convinced that I was simply stating the facts and fairly portraying the situation. It was a story that depicted me as a victim, and I didn't realize it until years later.

The choices we make in life bring us into situations that, for better or worse, can create experiences from which we can grow. Judging our circumstances moment by moment as good or bad is not the most effective way to live life. It is not what happens to you in life that matters but how you respond to it. This can seem a very easy statement to make from someone who has lived a fairly privileged life compared to others in the world. However, this is the philosophy and mindset that has led me out of the victim trap. These are beliefs that have helped me find the strength and confidence to succeed. Ultimately, this is a way of thinking that has allowed me to be happy, regardless of my circumstances.

Many years ago, a friend gave me a small book titled *Who Moved My Cheese?* by Spencer Johnson. It is a story in the form of a parable. One of the characters, named Hem, resists change and feels victimized in a "why is this happening to me" kind of way. The other character, named Haw, writes reminders on the walls of the maze they are in. They are reminders for himself. At one point, he writes the following question: "What would I do if I weren't afraid?" This question has helped me through many difficult choices in my life. If we identify as victims, we will be disempowered and live in fear.

When you think of a victim, what do you think of? Unless you are being victimized at this moment, are you a victim?

Karma and fate

If I don't believe in a deterministic universe, why consider such concepts as karma and fate? Perhaps because I see a benefit in imagining a process beyond our understanding or perception. It may help us make sense of our place in the world while influencing our response to the experiences life presents us with.

Like many of the words and concepts I have integrated into my philosophy, karma and fate are two words that I have defined in a way that is likely different from most people's interpretation. Many will see fate as those synchronistic moments we experience that significantly impact our lives. However, when we internalize our goals and vision for the future, our unconscious will provide the impulses, nudges, and intuitions that help guide us to exactly such moments. The traditional or esoteric definition of fate seems very deterministic, and I find it difficult to see any meaning or purpose in a life that is predetermined.

We are all born into a life containing elements out of our control. We are put on a path that has constraints and conditions but also opportunities and options. Some believe in divine interventions, where others see random chance. Whichever perspective serves you will not be right for others, but if there are invisible forces at work, they do not require a belief in them to function. Gravity and electricity work regardless of whether we believe in them or not. We only see their effects, but neither can be seen directly.

The definition of karma that works for me is best explained through an analogy. To me, karma is like a personal trainer for our growth. You may not appreciate all the workouts it puts you through, but sometimes on the journey of learning and enlightenment, the workout expression "no pain, no gain" rings very true. How much pain depends on the choices you make with the workouts you are given. Sometimes we just don't learn unless we are allowed to make the choices that help teach us, regardless of how painful they may be.

The choices you make in life indicate where you are on your path of growth in experience and understanding and therefore give rise to the karmic lessons you have yet to learn. Just as there are big and little lessons to learn, there are also varying degrees of karma depending on the scope of the lesson. I believe it is even possible that we have lived past lives or live in parallel experiences, creating karma that affects our entire lives or just stages of our lives: a year, a week, or a day.

In this way, I see karma as more of a universal education system rather than one of reward or punishment. I don't believe in good or bad karma. Instead, the choices you make daily are a reflection of past choices you have made and therefore indicate what you still have to learn. If you continue to make choices that display actions driven by fear rather than love, you will continue to ask karma to put you in situations which may be unpleasant. These situations will hopefully reflect to you the nature of your choices through their consequences.

My belief in such a karmic process encourages me to recognize thoughts and actions motivated by selfishness, greed, anger, hate, or any other fear-driven response to the world. I use this to hold myself accountable rather than looking for other people to blame. After all, I am the only one that I can control. Embracing this belief helps me to accept challenges or misfortunes in the spirit of growth and learning.

My view of fate is simply the conditions we are born into. We all start our journey through life under particular conditions, each with different opportunities to grow and learn. Regardless of your physical stature, gender, socio-economic status, or intellectual ability, each combination of traits and attributes has opportunities and challenges. If we embrace these conditions and see them as an opportunity, we can live life as Nietzsche recommended, embracing and loving our fate.

> *"May your choices reflect your hopes, not your fears."*
> - Nelson Mandela -

Questions

- Do you believe in free will? Does this belief serve you, your sense of purpose, your ability to take responsibility, your sense of hope, power, and confidence?
- Do you recognize choices that were pivotal in the direction of your life? Were any of these choices motivated by fear?
- Do you believe that you have the power to change your life?

9 MOTIVATION

"Don't be pushed around by the fears in your mind. Be led by the dreams in your heart."
- Roy T. Bennett -

As a coach, the topic of motivation inevitably comes up at some point when I'm working with clients. What is behind the actions and choices you make? How do you find the drive to pursue what you want in life? These are the two aspects of motivation that I want to cover in this chapter.

Motivation is also something we seek as if it were some kind of energy we can allocate to completing tasks and pursuing goals. We are driven by internal and external motivations, and knowing the difference is an important component of increasing happiness. If we need external impulses to motivate us, we will always be dependent on these conditions to take action. These external conditions may also influence us or cloud our judgement, making it difficult to recognize our own needs and desires. When we can identify what fulfills us and gives us a sense of purpose, motivation will come to us more easily.

For positive change to be possible, it is critical to have some clarity on what you want and what is needed to take action. If you can gain clarity around what is driving your choices and actions and recognize the beliefs, assumptions, and thinking habits that undermine your motivation, life becomes easier to navigate. By doing so, you will be closer to achieving your highest potential and living a more fulfilled life. This is the path to greater happiness.

It can be a challenge to recognize our physical, mental, or emotional needs and desires since most lie below the surface of our awareness. If we can recognize what our patterns of behaviour and mental strategies are trying to achieve, we can get closer to discovering what we truly want. Once this becomes clearer, we can determine whether what we want or our strategy for getting it has been driven by fear. In my philosophy, those actions motivated by fear eventually lead to outcomes that will not support our happiness and may even harm us or those around us.

Many things drive our choices and actions. The better we can understand our motivations, the better we will understand ourselves. This includes the strategies we have developed throughout our childhood, as well as beliefs that encourage us to rationalize our thoughts and assumptions. Understanding our motivations is challenging, especially considering the complex systems active on multiple levels. How are we supposed to recognize every biological, mental, and emotional need or desire that drives us at any given moment? Certainly, developing a higher sense of self-awareness is helpful in finding clues to this question. To help me find clarity, I have reduced motivation to a binary summed up by a simple question. Am I motivated by love or fear?

Motivation by fear

Until my early thirties, I was motivated mainly by fear. My choices were based on avoiding what I didn't want rather than pursuing what I did want. My life was guided by fear-based beliefs, leaving me with a sense of struggle and lack of abundance. In my distant past, I have told lies, been reckless, declined opportunities, and even stolen on a few occasions because of fear-based thinking. It has affected my relationships, my success, and my self-esteem. I didn't set out to hurt others, but I did.

When fear motivates us, it almost always leads to an outcome we do not want. We may have good intentions and want a positive outcome for ourselves or others, but when how we get there is driven by fear, the results are either negative or come at a high cost with negative side effects. When we are motivated by fear, it is the wrong time to take action.

A life lived in fear caused me to behave in opposition to my core values, which contributed to my unhappiness. But what does it mean to live in fear? Fear is not just what we are consciously afraid of. I didn't know I was acting out of fear. Most of the time, I didn't even recognize what I was afraid of. My fear of being alone or abandoned. My fear of not being good enough. My fear of not having enough or being poor. My fear of not being accepted or loved. These are just a few of the unconscious fears that motivated my actions for many years.

One of the most common behaviours we have that is motivated by fear is self-sabotage. In her book *Stop Self-Sabotage*, Dr. Judy Ho points out that our two primary drives in life are to gain rewards and avoid threats. Dr. Ho theorizes that self-sabotage is triggered by our desire to avoid threats such as, what if I don't succeed, what if I get rejected, and what if I am humiliated when I try something new? Threats invoke fear, so our response or strategy is motivated by fear. Contrary to Dr. Ho, I believe that our drive to gain rewards can also be fear-driven when we are motivated by such fear-based emotions as greed, insecurity, and envy.

In trying to better understand people, we may wonder what motivates them to do altruistic things or selfish acts. What motivates random acts of kindness to strangers or acts of violence towards fellow humans? I do not believe in evil but instead consider it an extreme form of fear. A desire for power, control, or domination can all be traced back to fear.

Over the past twenty years, I have become better at recognizing my fears and understanding how they motivate me. I have replaced old fear-based beliefs with more positive ones. My philosophy now contains new beliefs and positive strategies for responding to fear. This has allowed me to be motivated by my core values and my most authentic intentions. Through the context of love and fear, not only have my choices become clearer, but so has the motivation behind all that I do. When I have the clarity of mind to ask whether I am acting out of love or fear, I feel more in control of my thoughts and actions, as well as their outcomes.

Motivation by love

When helping someone who is ill or supporting a friend going through a difficult time, it may be easy to tell that you are motivated by love. The same is often true of parents with their children. However, there are many ways we can allow ourselves to be motivated by love in our everyday lives.

Every time we are truthful or forgiving, it is usually motivated by love. When we show gratitude and compassion, love is often the driver of such behaviour. Even when we are patient and forgiving toward ourselves, love is present. Love is often reflected in our actions when we are in a positive, joyful state. This is why I consider happiness such an important element of life. The more happiness we experience, the more we act out of love.

When you remove fear, it often allows room for love to motivate your actions. In my philosophy, love expresses itself naturally when fear is not present. It will then begin to inspire the thoughts, words, and actions of the higher self. This stems from my belief that love is our true nature when we are unaffected by fear. From this perspective, the more you overcome your fears, the more your words and actions will be driven by love.

Learning to recognize the nudges, thoughts, and intuitions that are born out of love takes practice in the same way that regaining your connection to your intuition requires repeated use. I find this way of defining what drives us into these two categories helps me to be aware of my motivations. Love motivates choices that support my happiness, and happiness helps me to act more out of love. With awareness and allowing, it is an upward spiral.

Intrinsic versus extrinsic motivation

Motivation is the drive to achieve or avoid an outcome. Psychology has identified two contrary influences or drivers of human motivation: intrinsic and extrinsic. When we are motivated intrinsically, we pursue activities out of our own curiosity or natural desire without the influence of external rewards. Extrinsic motivation is driven by external benefits such as reputation or financial gain. Those who are extrinsically motivated are often influenced by a desire to gain social approval and fit in. For this reason, intrinsic motivation is often seen as more positive and authentic. However, both have pros and cons, and we are usually influenced by a combination of the two.

An individual who is almost exclusively driven by intrinsic motivation will be very concerned with their own thoughts and feelings while having little awareness or even disregard for the needs of others or the impact of their actions on others. A person with strong intrinsic motivation may be seen as a free spirit but could also be narcissistic and socially awkward. They may have difficulty seeing the world from the perspective of other people and be very judgemental, seeing others as sheep or part of the herd.

People dominated by extrinsic motivation are primarily driven by external rewards and how others respond to them. Their personality and social strategies will be defined by external influences or interpretations of what they believe is expected or will bring them a desired external response. Such people may not have a clear sense of self or personal preferences. At some point, they may suffer from a crisis of identity but will seek external solutions for internal problems.

Extrinsic motivation can help you find success at work and, to some degree, in social networks. However, if intrinsic motivation—in other words, your inner needs and desires—are ignored, happiness will be elusive. Since we are social creatures, we tend to learn quickly to adopt behaviours that bring approval and other external repossess that we desire. For this reason, much of our behaviour is extrinsically motivated by a survival instinct. However, if we were raised with limited social contact, a lack of structure, and little feedback or guidance, we may end up at the other extreme. The more time we spend alone from a young age, the more foreign and awkward the outer social world will be for us. It is important for us to engage both of these drives to better navigate the world and find more happiness in doing so.

Some goals or tasks will be more affected by intrinsic or extrinsic forces. I write because I have something to say and want to help others. Some people set out to write a bestseller because of the credibility a book may provide. In my philosophy, I believe meaningful writing is better served by intrinsic motivation. However, I also have the extrinsic motivation to help and serve the needs of others with this book. When I coach or give workshops, I am primarily motivated by extrinsic forces. I seek financial reward and respond to the needs and wants of my clients. But I am also passionate about what I do, so there is also an intrinsic motivator in my work. I find this balance very positive.

Social media seems to be causing a stronger emphasis on extrinsic motivation. We behave or present ourselves in ways we expect will receive a desired response. Some will tell you to follow your dreams and passions, while others encourage you to be realistic. Success in life and happiness is best served by a combination of both. We need feedback from the systems surrounding us to make the best choices. This requires paying attention to the feedback from the external world, but if we live only by external feedback, we will not discover our highest potential or develop an authentic sense of self and will overlook the intuitive impulses that can help us make choices.

Our modern way of living presents us with many challenges when developing a healthy balance of intrinsic and extrinsic motivation. There are record numbers of people who feel isolated and alone. We live in opinion bubbles that reinforce our biases. Our mental models then become distorted and dysfunctional, as do the thoughts that grow from these perspectives. Add to this our non-stop access to digital screens selling us what we should want and need. These external stimuli make it more difficult to sort through the feelings, needs, and deeper desires below the surface.

Fear can be both intrinsic and extrinsic since we face external fears, as well as internal thoughts and beliefs. Love as a motivator is primarily internal; however, when we experience love from the external world, it also has a positive influence on us. This is my philosophy, and it helps me to be more aware of the motivations behind my thoughts, choices, and actions. Describing motivation in this way helps me gain a greater awareness of what is driving me. This gives me greater control of myself and allows for greater happiness.

The power of intention

I believe intention matters, but not in the way that someone like American philosopher Sam Harris seems to refer to it—as a justification for doing bad things to achieve "good" outcomes. Some would argue that intentions do not matter and only outcomes matter. In my philosophy, intention and outcome are deeply connected. If we are not clear on our intentions, our actions and choices may be chaotic and reactive.

Knowing the reason you want something is important. It is understanding where the desire is coming from and what motivates it. Here again, I use my foundation. Is my intention driven by love or fear? Is this intention influenced by my ego? What is the strategy I am following? Our strategies always have intentions.

If there is a universal or collective consciousness, does it have an intention? Carlos Castaneda writes, "In the universe, there is an immeasurable, indescribable force which shamans call intent, and absolutely everything that exists in the entire cosmos is attached to intent by a connecting link." Wayne Dyer also spoke about intention not being something you have but something you tap into. I imagine my intuition and the signals I receive as having an intention. When my body creates a fever or has an autoimmune response, it has an intention.

When we understand what part of us is driving an intention, it becomes easier to understand if this aligns with what we actually want to achieve. This clarity around why we want to take action will help us find the motivation around how to take action.

I have already mentioned the power we have when we internalize thoughts and beliefs. The more we clarify and internalize our intentions, the more power and clarity our actions will have. With clarity in our consciousness, the outcomes of our actions will help us match or exceed the expectations of our original intention.

Understanding needs

Almost eighty years have passed since Abraham Maslow presented his theory of what motivates human behaviour, known as Maslow's Hierarchy of Needs. I like his theory because it combines the physical, mental, and spiritual needs we all have. Some people approach life with a pragmatic strategy for survival and external success, while others are willing to sacrifice physical comforts to pursue a more spiritual path. Maslow addresses both our basic human needs and our higher aspirations.

The Hierarchy of Needs is modelled as a pyramid with five levels beginning with the base needs at the foundation and the more aspirational needs at the peak. The first category describes our physiological needs. These include the need for food, water, and sexual reproduction. In other words, these are our essential physical needs. The second level refers to security and safety needs. Now we are already in the territory of mind since we have both mental and physical security needs. In the middle of the pyramid is love and belonging. These are the mental and emotional needs for love and community. If these levels are fulfilled, anyone can live comfortably, but the pyramid does not stop there.

Human beings also have spiritual needs, which we often ignore in an effort to fulfill our base needs. The fourth level in Maslow's hierarchy is esteem. At this level, it is not enough to be accepted. We seek the approval, respect, and even admiration of others. These may sound like the needs of the ego, but only when driven by fear or a sense of lack. The feedback we get from others helps in our spiritual desire for growth.

Finally, the top of the hierarchy is called self-actualization. I consider this the pursuit of one's highest potential. At this point, we are motivated by the spiritual element of our human experience. These are the growth and awareness that I believe lead to life's greatest joy and authentic happiness. However, I do not encourage people to see this as a hill to climb or a path to follow. These needs are active in us at all times. Our physical needs remain, even as we seek self-actualization. One could easily put these needs in five categories without the pyramid, but this model helps us visualize the difficulty in growing in relationships, esteem, and self-actualization when we are hungry and afraid for our future. The model also helps us recognize the difference between surviving and thriving.

Numerous psychologists have adopted or built upon Maslow's theory, but more recent research around motivation in the workplace also seems to confirm the needs at higher levels in the hierarchy. Daniel Pink breaks down some of this research in his book Drive. For years, companies have been trying to motivate people through financial incentives, which often do not motivate people toward the desired outcomes. It seems these rewards only work with simple tasks that do not require any creative thinking. In our modern world of work, such jobs are in the minority. Applied in the modern workplace, pressure tied to such incentives often causes people to underperform while others lose sight of their values and use poor judgement in making decisions. Incentives that speak to our base needs can trigger fear. This means the old carrot and stick model of motivation is no longer relevant in our modern world.

Daniel Pink presents a model that increases motivation when our base needs are met. When food, shelter, and safety are not an issue—or as Pink describes it, when money is off the table—three factors most impact a person's motivation. The first is autonomy. This is tied to our need for a sense of independence and self-direction. Autonomy gives us the sense that we have some control over the outcome of our actions and the direction of our lives. This creates higher levels of engagement and satisfaction at work.

Mastery is the second category, which relates to our desire for growth. When we engage in activities that make us feel that we continue to learn and grow, we will be more motivated. The third pillar of this model is purpose. When we understand what our contribution is to a greater goal or outcome, we are more motivated. When we are part of a cause we believe in, it gives us a sense of purpose, and we are more motivated. These three pillars of motivation can be applied to work or any other goals we aspire to. In anything we want to accomplish, if we have the same degree of autonomy in how it gets done, learn new skills or gain new experiences, and find meaning in what we are doing, the conditions for motivation are optimal.

We all have needs, and when we are aware of these, it may make it easier to understand our motivations. When we add fear to the equation, it may result in attempts to fulfill our needs through selfish or reckless ways. When our physical, mental, and spiritual needs are met, it becomes easier to let love be our primary motivation.

Overcoming resistance

What is your biggest obstacle in achieving your goals and achieving your potential? For the majority of people, there is only one correct answer here. The answer is you. There may be circumstances out of your control and challenges you cannot avoid, but these are not the biggest obstacles. In my experience, the biggest obstacles most people face are those they create for themselves.

In this book, we are working through the beliefs and thinking habits that stand in our way. This is also what stands in the way of your motivation. Originally, I considered the biggest obstacle we have in life to be fear, but ultimately, it is how we address or process fear that inevitably determines whether it is an obstacle. Once you recognize and acknowledge that you are the one standing in your own way, you can start to develop strategies to overcome your obstacles.

Growing up, I was constantly told how lazy I was. It was meant to motivate me, but it did the opposite. I started to believe it was true. It became part of my identity, and I thought I was just born lazy. There were times I worked really hard to prove I was not lazy, while other times I felt my in-born laziness was insurmountable and thus gave in to it. As already discussed, what was later identified as depression was something I thought was just laziness. Clearly, I was poorly informed and came to some odd conclusions. We all have erroneous beliefs about ourselves, mostly negative, and these create endless obstacles to our motivation.

Needless to say, I no longer believe in laziness. We are not lazy; we only lack motivation. If I feel lazy, that's fine. It is just describing the state I am in. But laziness as a character trait is inaccurate and unhelpful. Motivation is something you can take control of, whereas laziness can feel like something you are afflicted with.

Procrastination is often considered a form of laziness, but in some cases, it is actually a stress response. It may be a sign that you feel overwhelmed, or maybe you are afraid of failing. Any number of fears could be behind the reason you are procrastinating. It may also be that a task is framed in a negative way, causing you to avoid it unnecessarily. How we view ourselves, how we interpret the tasks at hand, and what we believe about ourselves all influence our ability to become motivated.

Some feel motivation is overrated. These people will tell you that all you need is discipline. While this may work for some, for many, it does not; when they fail, they feel guilty, ashamed, and discouraged. I don't believe in discipline. The word conjures images of a life lived with many restrictions and punishment for disobeying. I do, however, believe in willpower and determination. Everything in this chapter has been geared to help you become more aware of the what and how of motivation. Recognizing the fears and negative beliefs that undermine your motivation is the first step to change. This will allow your motivation to be driven by your needs, values, and ultimately, by love.

An important point about how we frame situations is the language we use. We often speak in terms of obligation. I should do this or I have to do that. If you were anything like me as a teenager, when your parents told you what you had to do, you might have wanted to avoid it or do the opposite. I didn't like the feeling of being forced to do something. It created resistance in me. When you use words like I have to, I must, or I should, this obligation may also trigger resistance in you. There are three ways to talk about your tasks: I can, I want to, and I will. You can even ask yourself these questions when embarking on a task. Can I? Do I want to? Will I? In other words: Do I have the ability, do I have the desire, and will I commit to this task? When you use I can, I want to, or I will to describe your plans or intentions, resistance will be reduced because you are taking ownership using your free will.

As a final note, I would like to point to the conditions that will help you overcome the resistance that stands in the way of your motivation. I once again refer to psychologist Mihaly Csikszentmihalyi who pioneered the research around flow. Flow is a term Csikszentmihalyi adopted for his theories because it is how his test subjects often referred to their experience. In the flow state, a person is so focused and involved in what they are doing that there is no distraction or resistance from inner or outer stimuli. This means their thoughts and external influences are temporarily tuned out. In the flow state, we lose our sense of time, concentration is effortless, and anything outside of our focus becomes irrelevant. I have heard athletes and musicians talk about this state in terms of being "in the zone."

Csikszentmihalyi's model for achieving flow involves a balance of challenge and skill. If a task is too challenging, we may become frustrated or anxious; if it is too easy, we may become bored. Apathy is also an enemy of flow. If we do not care and are not invested in the journey or the outcome, it will not be possible to experience flow. The state of flow is achieved as we do the things we love to do and continue to challenge ourselves to get better. In this way, I consider it a love state. The positive energy that drives us to pursue the growth, learning, and achievement of our full potential is, for me, a form of love.

Csikszentmihalyi also points out the role happiness plays in this state. He tells us, "A man can make himself happy or miserable, regardless of what is actually happening `outside` just by changing the contents of his consciousness."

It's interesting that we primarily think about motivation when it is missing. Rarely do people consider motivation when they are feeling very driven to do something. In the flow state, motivation is never in question. Where do you see an abundance of motivation? When people have purpose and passion? When they are free to pursue what fulfills them? I see it in small children. They do not need motivation to jump out of bed and start their day. They are often curious and looking for things to do as soon as they wake up. Children are not encumbered by the past. What does this tell you? Find your curiosity and your optimism. Turn work into play, and try to spend more time seeing the world through your inner child's eyes.

Questions
- When you think of some of the most important actions you have taken or choices you have made, what was the main motivation driving them?
- In what situations do you feel a sense of motivation or drive to complete a task? Do you know what conditions need to be met for you to feel motivated?
- Do you feel resistance to accomplish the things you want to achieve in your life?
- Is there something you fear will happen?
- What will change if you achieve the goals you set for yourself?
- Can you see any hidden benefit in not accomplishing what you desire?

10 THE PRESENT

"When you are present in this moment, you break the continuity of your story, of past and future. Then true intelligence arises, and also love."
- Eckhart Tolle -

We live each moment of our physical lives anchored in the present, but so much of our conscious awareness is focused away from this reality. Our minds take us away from the now and move our attention to the past or the future. Authentic happiness is in the present moment. Anything else is memory or anticipation, but even these we experience in the present moment. Our power to choose and act is also in the present. Therefore a return to the now will help us take back our power. In this chapter, I will build upon ideas from previous chapters, such as behaviour, thinking, and choices, in an endeavour to help you recognize more fully what it means to be present.

The teachings of Eckhart Tolle have had a significant impact on me. His book *The Power of Now* made a lasting impression, as have his many talks. Perhaps one of the most intriguing things I have ever heard him say was that many people live as if the present moment were an obstacle they need to overcome. This has certainly been true for me at times. It is true of anyone who makes if /then statements, such as if I meet the right person, then I'll be happy. Or if I get a good job, then I will feel successful. One of my statements was, "When I know enough, then I will continue writing my book." I will never know enough, but what I know now is worth something to me and, hopefully, others. When the success and happiness we desire are somewhere in some undefined place in the future, what does that leave us with in the present?

The present moment is not an obstacle, but it is an opportunity. What we are experiencing now is largely the result of all of our past choices and actions. It can be difficult to recognize that all of your power, potential, and happiness are only available to you in this moment. What about past circumstances that robbed you of potential opportunities? What about the goals and dreams you are striving for? None of it matters if you do not allow the awareness you need to recognize where you stand now.

The moments of joy, awe, and inspiration we experience happen expressly in the now. Attempts at achieving peak performance through the flow state involve being in the now. Special moments of happiness, deep engagement with others, and opportunities for change are all undermined by our lack of presence. But what about learning from the past and planning for the future? Both reflection and planning are actions we take in the now. If you reflect or plan without being clearly anchored in the present with an awareness of where you stand now, these efforts will be ineffective.

Who you are now is also unique to this moment. Physically, the cells in your body have died and been replaced many times over, so you no longer have the same body you had five or ten years ago. Your experiences have led to new thoughts, and although many of us develop repetitive thinking habits as we get older, everything from the way we experience time to the way we remember the past changes over time. Those we consider wise are often older. So, although we age and our physical apparatus degrades, the mind can continue to evolve. Spiritually, we also mature and grow through our experiences and the ability to heal, overcome trauma, and process fear. Who you are now may not exist in the same way next week, so there may be important opportunities to experience at this moment.

What are you aware of at this moment? How does it feel to be you right now? How can you spend more moments anchored in the present? What does it even mean to be present? As you read on, I hope I can point you in the right direction to answer these questions for yourself.

Mindfulness

The experience of being fully present used to happen to me unintentionally and infrequently. It was not until I began practicing meditation that I gained an understanding and awareness of what being present feels like. To be more present longer, it is helpful to meditate regularly and develop a mindfulness practice. Mindfulness means different things to different people, and I will share some definitions provided by some great thinkers on this topic. Ideally, the way mindfulness is described in this section will help you understand the state of mind you are looking for. From there, you will be able to define it for yourself.

It's interesting to me that to practice mindfulness, it is helpful to distance ourselves from the mind. Or at least to step back from the mental chatter generated by the mind. This is the confusion sometimes created by the words we use, especially when translating from other languages. Mindfulness comes from the word *sati*, as it is used in Buddhism, which is interpreted as "deep remembrance." Meditation creates a similar issue in English since it is also often used to refer to a form of contemplation, which is the opposite of the Eastern practice we attempt to understand in the West.

I will share a few interpretations to help you find a suitable definition for your philosophy. John Vervaeke, PhD in Philosophy and lecturer at the University of Toronto, takes a scientific approach to many spiritual practices. He is a long-time practitioner and lecturer on mindfulness, and he sees the practice in terms of perception or framing of experience. His technical definition of mindfulness is as follows: Mindfulness is frame awareness that can be appropriated in order to improve your capacities for insight and self-regulation. John Kabat-Zinn describes it this way: Mindfulness is an awareness that arises through paying attention, on purpose, in the present moment, non-judgementally.

Eckhart Tolle refers to presence as something that finds you and flows through you. To find presence through mindfulness, he recommends noticing the gaps between thoughts. When we focus on the space between our thoughts, says Tolle, a new level of awareness can arise.

My own definition describes mindfulness as the act of observing life with a high level of awareness, allowing us to experience each moment more fully. I have a sense of what this means to me, but for anyone else, it only points to the meaning. All of these above definitions, including mine, point to a feeling, a state, or a way of being, and it is important to choose a definition or description that best helps you find this experience.

When you find a definition that suits you, the instructions for being mindful will be within that description. Start with activities where you find it easy to be mindful, in other words, fully aware of the present moment. For me, this includes simple things that I do regularly, like walking, cooking, and washing the dishes. If you need more instructions than this, Thích Nhất Hạnh provides three easy steps you can apply to any situation where you want to be more mindful: pause, breathe, smile.

Releasing trauma

If there is one thing that keeps us bound to the past and negatively impacts our present life, it is trauma. We cannot truly release our past until we heal our past trauma. If we can't release our past, it will be difficult to live fully in the present. No matter the conditions of your present moment, trauma will affect your capacity for happiness.

Trauma is not what happens to you. It's what happens inside you. These are the words of Dr. Gabor Mate, and this is important because if trauma was about what happened to you, it would stop when the traumatic experience stops. Instead, the traumas of the past plague us because they continue to live inside us. Through his work, Mate explores the connection between trauma and the many dysfunctions and diseases we experience in society. He also works with people suffering from addiction in the city where I grew up, Vancouver, Canada.

As an expert in trauma and how to heal from it, Gabor Mate sees the connection between trauma and physical illness. He also promotes educating everyone—from teachers to physicians—about trauma as a way of healing society. I think that trauma keeps a great deal of fear anchored in each of us, and when I see people acting in negative ways, I see fear in them. In perhaps a similar way, Mate sees trauma as the source of the dysfunction and addictive behaviour in people and society at large.

For many years, I saw myself as flawed and somehow broken, but I believed I was born this way. There was nothing in my childhood that I considered terribly traumatic, especially when compared to some of the difficult childhoods other people have suffered through. Looking back with the help of a therapist, although my adult perspective didn't identify trauma, to a child experiencing the events of my young life, it may have felt traumatic. For example, Gabor Mate points out the effect of adults' stress and anxiety on babies and young children. If our parents or primary caregivers experienced stressful life events when we were very young, this may have had a lasting emotional impact on us. This is especially true of those like me who are more sensitive or who were sensitive children. Many of us may still carry emotionally charged events of our past within our psyche. This is why it is important not to downplay the fears, anxiety, and other emotions that keep you tied to events of your past. Trauma keeps part of us tethered to the past, and this connection cannot be broken without healing.

Finding ways to let go of those events that tie us to the past can free us from chains we didn't know held us back. Unfortunately, many people may bury their traumas beneath habits and distractions. Others may embrace their role as a victim without actually trying to heal and overcome their trauma. Faced with physical trauma, I assume most people would seek out a medical practitioner who would assist in healing their body. Why should it be any different when healing psychological or emotional trauma?

Without doing the work and finding ways to heal your emotional traumas, those parts of your past will continue to influence your present thoughts, feelings, and actions, no matter how long ago they happened. If you want to identify what is holding you back from living a life where you are truly present, it is important to see the world through the lens of past traumas. This is not to say we should forget our past, but instead, we can release the emotional burden of such events to allow us to view them more objectively from the present. In this way, we can find more happiness in the present moment.

Forgiveness

What does it mean for you to forgive someone? Do you release the one you are forgiving from responsibility? Do you even need to inform the person you are forgiving? You may want to inform someone to forgive them, but ultimately the act of forgiveness is something you do for yourself. This is the irony of the way most people perceive forgiveness. The less we are willing to forgive, the more we are bound to or burdened by the person or act we refuse to forgive. Refusing to forgive someone is similar to the way we disempower ourselves by identifying as a victim. We keep ourselves stuck in the painful or unhappy events of the past.

I try to hold to a philosophy that recognizes we are all doing the best we can with the knowledge and experience we currently have. I remind myself of this when I think of negative experiences with my parents. I try to remember this when thinking of any number of past events where I was cheated, robbed, betrayed, or in some way treated unjustly. This philosophy helps me forgive and let go. Letting go through the act of forgiveness allows us to live more in the present and be less burdened by the past.

The act of forgiving is not only meant for others. Sometimes the person we most need to forgive is ourselves. When we live a life of guilt and regret, we may undermine our potential and even become self-destructive, but we often also may cause hurt and suffering to others. I am sure many alcoholics and drug addicts are burdened by guilt and regret. I also lived with a great deal of guilt and regret for most of my life, which negatively affected my relationships and people relying on me. Not forgiving yourself will not benefit anyone else, even if you caused harm to them in the past. There are constructive ways to make amends or repay a debt, but guilt and regret are not part of the solution. They are fear-based emotions that keep us stuck in the past.

Just as trauma requires healing, so does any kind of emotional pain from past experiences. Whether you are trying to forgive yourself or someone else, there is likely some emotional pain that requires healing before forgiveness is possible. The healing process is a matter of releasing the pain and fear associated with the past. I am not going to provide techniques for healing because this is not my area of expertise. This work is best done with the help of a good therapist or through a program that supports emotional healing. I would point out that events in our past that require our forgiveness have also caused us to develop beliefs that stand in the way of our progress.

If you can let go of beliefs that are based on blame, resentment, guilt, or regret, you will aid your healing process and allow yourself to let go of the past. You can find these beliefs within the stories you tell yourself and others about your past. If you were abused, grew up with an alcoholic parent, were bullied at school, lived through difficult experiences, were cheated on, did things you are ashamed of, and continue to tell this story about yourself, you are living in the past. When you forgive the past, you can let go of your story and, in doing so, start to live a better life in the present.

Planning and worry

When we plan, we do it in the present. The reason we plan is to help us make better decisions in the present. It helps give our life direction and purpose. Planning for the future informs the actions we take and what we seek to learn in the current moment. The act of planning is almost like a feedback loop from the future as we imagine the outcome of our current actions. When we imagine the future and experience the present, it is all happening now.

Planning allows us to create opportunities because we have the capacity to imagine the future. Issues arise when we become more focused on the future or perhaps even obsessed with a particular outcome. When we are so focussed on the future, we are susceptible to overlooking opportunities or challenges in the present moment. Sometimes we outright ignore the issues in the present because we are so focussed on a future outcome.

As we develop plans and expectations for the future, we may become worried about the results or outcomes of our actions. This may be based on past failures or just on our insecurities. Worry is also something we do in the now, but it is unproductive and keeps our focus where we have no power: in the future. Our power is only in the now.

My philosophy does focus heavily on my ongoing development

and learning, but it is not in pursuit of some future outcome. I don't know where my growth and learning will lead. I have no expectations of enlightenment, only ongoing improvement. I reflect and plan, but I am aware that I do these from my perspective in the now. The plans I want to achieve and the things I want to learn and grow from will be diminished if I am focused on their achievement.

Before becoming aware of my struggles with staying present, I would spend a lot of time dreaming about the future without taking any action, only to one day realize that the opportunity for action had passed. Others might be very successful but sacrificed personal relationships or experiences that might have made their lives fuller and more balanced because they didn't step back and become more fully aware of the present moment.

If your philosophy contains beliefs about a constant striving for the future, you may not be allowing yourself to fully experience the present. When moving to Europe, the city that had in part inspired my move was Hamburg, Germany. There was something about the city that drew me to it and made me feel at home. A little more than a year after moving to Hamburg, I relocated to Munich for a job. Munich is a nice city, but it didn't inspire me the way Hamburg did, so I quickly decided this would be temporary. For most of the four and half years I lived there, I was focused on leaving the city and moving back to Hamburg. Looking back, I realize I never really appreciated or fully took advantage of all that I could have experienced in Munich. There was a belief in my philosophy that I am not sure I can even describe now, but I felt that I could not be content with my current situation, as it might make me complacent about change. I was so focused on looking for a plan to leave that I wasn't fully living in the present.

Focus and distraction

Although I have already written about distraction, this kind of distraction is different. Distraction as a strategy for avoiding negative thoughts and feelings is an intentional strategy or coping mechanism. At least it starts as intentional and then becomes a habit or even an addiction. This is, however, another kind of distraction. It is unintentional and causes our focus to drift away from experiencing life in the moment.

For as long as I can remember, I have had difficulty with focus. As a child at school, it was a rare report card that didn't have some comment along the lines of "Peter is easily distracted." Since then, I have struggled to concentrate on everything from reading a book to having a conversation. Sometimes my mind jumps around in a conversation, making connections that other people can't follow because I've shifted to something not necessarily relevant to the topic at hand. At times, I set off to do something or get something, only to forget what it was. I will start something, forgetting that I have not yet completed my previous task. I used to frequently get frustrated with myself and my inability to remember things or stay on track.

It could be that I suffer from some type of executive dysfunction or attention deficit disorder, but such a diagnosis does not help me get closer to a solution. It only leads to prescriptions that treat symptoms. This is not medical advice; it is my philosophy and may not be right for others. I am more interested in what I consider lasting solutions that do not require a lifetime of medication. Thankfully, my meditation, mindfulness practice, and other work I have done to improve my focus have helped, so I can be fully present for my coaching clients and other important people in my life. Over the past twenty years, I have improved greatly, although I still have my moments of frustration. With the right practices, anyone can improve their ability to focus and concentrate.

In the busy world we live in, with an abundance of stimuli and demands for our attention, it is easy to understand why we may become distracted from the present moment and what is important to us. We have so much to occupy our minds that when this stimulus stops, we may have difficulty dealing with the peace and silence of the present moment. It can feel so foreign to us that it makes us uncomfortable. However, it is exactly these moments, focused on the space between our thoughts or the goings on around us, that we need to allow for more presence. Instead, we become distracted without noticing.

In his 2019 TED Talk about how mindfulness changes the emotional life of our brains, Prof. Richard Davidson discusses research that indicates distracted people are unhappy people. One of the studies found that Americans spent 47 per cent of their time not focused on what they were doing. From personal experience, I suspect this number would likely increase for anyone suffering from depression or anxiety disorder. I spent my teens and twenties with the vast majority of my focus not on the present moment. If we combine intentional and unintentional distractions, I imagine there are people who exceed 70 per cent of their time not focused on the present. Naturally, the type of work that one does will play a role. If your job does not require you to be mentally engaged because it is just an automated set of procedures that you feel you could do in your sleep, there is a lot of opportunity for your mind to wander away from the present.

Systemic principles encourage us to zoom in and out to help us gain perspective on the complex systems we are trying to understand. Life is the most complex system we will ever experience. When thinking of focus, we might relate this more to zooming in and looking closely at details, but there is focus in zooming out as well. When you look through a camera lens and zoom out, you can still see things clearly, but you see a much broader picture. This kind of focus is not about noticing details but instead about seeing the big picture. Practicing the ability to zoom out and just take in the present moment without focusing on any particular thought or detail will allow new things into your awareness, sometimes helping you notice things you overlooked before. It will help you be more aware of the present moment.

The benefits of presence

Since happiness is only in the present, whether it comes from a memory, the anticipation of the future, or an experience in the now, the primary benefit of being present is the opportunity for happiness. The less we regret the past or worry about the future, the more we will find opportunities for happiness. In my view, this in itself is a great benefit. But wait, there's more!

The opportunity for change is also in the present. We often remember the momentous life-changing experiences that we've had, but there will be far more tiny events that have accumulated to create considerably more significant changes in our life. I consider my six-month backpacking trip through Asia to have been life-changing, but there was not one major experience that I can point to. I remember narrowly missing getting crushed by a boulder in a landslide travelling by road from Tibet to Nepal. I remember breathtaking views. I remember hours spent at my hut on the beach in Vietnam, writing every morning. It was an accumulation of many special and sometimes even challenging moments. What I do know is that when arriving in Germany after six months in Asia, I had a calm and sense of presence I had not previously achieved. The lasting change that happens in ourselves is through small behavioural changes that accumulate into significant outcomes in the long term. When we are present, we can realize more of these opportunities for change.

Awareness allows change and allows for a more helpful and positive philosophy. The act of being present in our physical, mental, and spiritual selves naturally creates a higher level of awareness. Although it is our minds that tend to draw us into the past or the future, our bodies and emotional selves can also be tied to the past. As Dr. Joe Dispenza discusses in his book *Breaking the Habit of Being Yourself*, we practice emotional responses to situations that we learned from our past and may no longer be relevant or necessary in the present. These practiced emotions are tied to chemical or hormonal responses in the body. When we heal the body, mind, and spirit and bring our awareness into the present, we experience life more fully and with less fear.

Finally, all of our power is in the now. It follows then that the more present we are, the more empowered we will be. What happens in your future is far more about the decisions you make in the present. Everything else is out of your control anyway. Whatever plans or dreams you have, the first step is taken now. You cannot "should have" done anything. You either did something or did not. Should is a past opportunity that you did not pursue. You can only take action in the now. With this in mind, remember that the most powerful tool for clarity you can have in the present is to pause, breathe, and be fully in the moment. In such moments, the insights and inspirations you allow space for can be life-changing.

In a moment of presence, we can temporarily be free from some of our mental habits and fears. Under such conditions, we can be far more creative and insightful, but we also have a far higher capacity for assessing situations and solving problems. Being present is therefore one of the best ways to experience your full potential.

> *"Realize deeply that the present moment is all you ever have."*
> - Eckhart Tolle -

The past is only reference material, and the future is the blank page, so the opportunity you have is to spend each day writing the best story that you can. If we consider ourselves writers of our own stories, we will live from the perspective of creators of our own lives.

The past then becomes an accumulation of experiences that have made us who we are at this moment but do not limit what we can be tomorrow.

Questions
- Based on what you have read in this chapter, can you recognize what it feels like to be fully present?
- If so, when was the last time you felt fully present in the moment? What conditions helped you give your full attention to the moment?
- What most often takes you out of the present moment? For example, regret, worry, daydreaming, reminiscing, thinking about the future, rerunning past evenings in your mind?
- What are the moments that you would really like to be present for?

11 RELATIONSHIPS

"The quality of our relationships determines the quality of our lives."
- Esther Perel -

The complexity of relationships is, in my view, the most important element of the human experience to understand. On every level of our experience, we have a fundamental need for connection. On a physical level, we have a need for touch, and our health benefits from such contact. Mentally we possess a deep desire for connection, without which we feel lonely and isolated. When our needs for belonging and connection are not fulfilled, our mental health suffers tremendously. Spiritually we all need to be loved and long for an emotional sense of community. My view is that our connections to others create opportunities for spiritual growth and a form of learning that is only possible through interactions with particular people. Even if you do not share my spiritual views, it is clear that through our ability to interact with others, we learn more about ourselves and our place in the world.

As I have already mentioned, I consider systemic thinking extremely beneficial for engaging with the world and essential for understanding the complexity of life. One of the most important systemic principles is recognizing relationships within complex systems. Human relationships are the most complex systems we interact with, and our ability to understand these relationships is key to our success and happiness. Unfortunately, we rarely look at relationships systemically. We look at behaviours or what people say and make judgements from there. We look for the good and the bad or the right and the wrong as we observe or interact with others. Our emotions draw us into situations, making it difficult to be objective.

Beliefs about relationships are perhaps some of the first ideas we adopt from the time of birth. Early on, we develop strategies based on these beliefs and perceptions as we engage with the people around us. In this chapter, we will look at relationships from a variety of perspectives to help you decide which beliefs can help bring more harmony and fulfillment to your life. I will not, however, give any advice. I am not an expert in this area and have had my fair share of challenges in personal and professional relationships. I will share what I have learned and reflected on, but my growth in this area, more than any other, is ongoing.

The nature of relationships

I started this chapter with a few thoughts on why it is so important to understand relationships and clarify our beliefs around them. In this section, I would like to consider the purpose they may serve. There are solitary mammals on our planet who thrive living independently from others of their species. Bears, skunks, and leopards are just a few examples of animals that are loners. Naturally, some individual humans can live alone and prefer such a lifestyle. For the vast majority of us, however, this is not the case. Why do humans find it so necessary to create a network of connections with other humans and sometimes animals?

As much as my philosophy considers the spiritual nature of relationships, I have considered this topic from many perspectives.

However, I recognize that the way we act in relationships is often driven by learned patterns of behaviour and instinctual impulses that evolved over time. I will use my usual three levels of human experience to consider more closely the nature of relationships.

From a biological perspective, we have evolved to seek connection with others. Evolutionary theory indicates that natural selection has caused our biology to adapt in ways that influence how we interact with other people. This would mean that our genetics have geared us toward everything, from the way we choose a romantic partner to the complexities of our social networks. The evolutionary process is, in basic terms, a cost-benefit analysis. Relationships, therefore, according to evolutionary theory, must have a benefit for the survival of our genes, which are greater than any cost associated with pursuing them.

Clearly, our biology is geared toward bonding and connection with others. The brain produces oxytocin, which plays a role in social bonding, and other mechanisms in the body also support cooperation and the forming of relationships. People give blood, donate organs, and even sacrifice themselves for others in acts that do not seem selfish or self-serving, although evolutionary theorists also have an explanation for this cost-benefit analysis. Are relationships simply driven by some genetic strategy to achieve the greatest benefit at the lowest cost?

We have a psychological need for connection to others. Although there are a few outliers, people generally cannot thrive in isolation. This may be difficult to disconnect from our biological impulses, but there is clearly a mental component to relationships. Many of our behaviours in relationships stem from the way we perceive the outside world and our connection to it. We develop mental strategies around how to navigate relationships based on early experiences, which can remain with us for a lifetime. Depending on our experiences in those formative years, some strategies will be beneficial, while others will cause us to struggle in certain types of relationships.

Behavioural economists see our behaviour and interactions through the lens of our psychological motivations and strategies. Unlike classical economics, these theories do not assume that individuals are thinking rationally or acting in their best interest. These theories are sometimes used to observe and understand human relationships. There may be a benefit to viewing human interactions from the perspective of an idea such as Game Theory, but I find that many such theories project a very selfish and even negative image of human relationships. These beliefs lead to a view of relationships as a means to an end rather than an opportunity for human exploration and emotional fulfillment.

In his book *Games People Play*, psychiatrist Dr. Eric Berne outlines his theory of transactional analysis. Transactional analysis is an interesting way to reflect on our relationships and the interactions that we have. It is a great tool for reflection and self-awareness, which helps us understand why we assume different roles in different relationships. But what does this tell us about the nature of relationships other than that they are complex and sometimes difficult to navigate?

Empirical science has greatly increased our knowledge and ability to manipulate the physical world, mostly for our benefit. Unfortunately, I find it falls short of helping us understand the human experience on an emotional level. It is difficult to fully understand the nature of relationships without considering the mental and emotional impact and benefit of the relationships we engage in. Are the physical and mental benefits we gain and the social connections we require to thrive simply part of our physical evolution? Or is there an emotional and spiritual evolution also at play? I believe it is our spiritual nature to grow and evolve through the wide range of physical, intellectual, and emotional experiences that we have throughout our lifetime. This is one of my core beliefs about the nature of relationships.

There are physical reasons we are attracted to another person, just as there are mental aspects to attraction. We are physically drawn to aspects of the human anatomy for the evolutionary benefits of passing on our genes. Mentally, we may have patterns of behaviour or aspects of personality that we are drawn to. But relationships evoke feelings and emotions, which I often consider from a spiritual perspective. Beyond the basic benefits of cooperation, we learn and grow from the relationships we engage in. These lessons can be happy, joyful, or painful, but they are always useful, assuming we have the awareness to grow from them.

Relationship strategies

When I speak to parents or observe them interacting with their young children, they are aware of their kids' simple strategies or attempts to manipulate people. Some people also recognize such patterns in the behaviour of adults with whom they have a relationship. However, if I asked any of these people to identify some of their strategies in relationships, many would struggle to come up with even a few examples. Understanding the strategies at play in relationships, whether our own or other people's, will help us change our behaviour and become less reactive to the behaviour of others.

From an early age, we interpret the world and develop strategies around how to navigate life, learning how to get what we want or need. In other words, we develop beliefs about life, and our strategies are then based on these beliefs. This is not limited to relationships, but our strategies in relationships will often explain a great deal about how people respond to and interact with us.

Many of our strategies in life are fear-based. Rather than looking for ways to get what we want and need, we develop strategies to avoid loss, mitigate risk, and avoid failure. When we attempt to manipulate people through deception to get what we want, this is also a form of fear. We may often be unaware of employing such strategies, to the degree that we would even deny them when they are pointed out to us.

There are two distinct problems I observe with many of the strategies people use based on past experience. Often, the strategies from our past are no longer relevant or appropriate for our current situation. When I see an adult lose their temper in an immature way, I wonder about which childhood strategy is currently at play. Was this someone who would have a temper tantrum as a child when they didn't get what they wanted?

If you experienced trauma as a child, this may have also led to unhelpful strategies in your adult relationships. Such strategies do not just come from childhood. If you went through a painful breakup, felt betrayed, or experienced negative behaviour from an intimate partner, you will naturally want to make sure you avoid this in future relationships. You then develop strategies based on that previous relationship, but people are different and not all relationships are the same. Using strategies from past relationships in new ones could really undermine their potential. If you were lied to, deceived, or taken advantage of in a past relationship and your strategy is to no longer trust people you are emotionally involved with, your relationships will struggle to find happiness and harmony.

In a talk given by Simon Sinek, he asks the question, "Do you know what all of my failed relationships have in common?" His answer? "Me." If you find yourself continually experiencing similar unhappy outcomes in your professional or personal relationships, it may be time to ask what you are contributing to the outcomes in these relationships. Within our patterns of behaviour, it may be possible to recognize strategies that can point to beliefs that are not helping you. The partners we choose, the people we feel drawn to, our responses to certain situations, how we deal with conflicts, and many other conscious and unconscious behaviours can be part of your relationship strategies. Discovering your strategies, like identifying your philosophy, will lead to happier relationships.

Attachment theory

Attachment theory highlights the long-lasting effects of our early attachments with our closest caregivers early in life. To better understand our behaviour in our closest relationships, I would take this theory a little further. Recognizing these patterns in ourselves can better inform our beliefs about relationships.

The first ideas around attachment theory were developed by British psychologist John Bowlby, who viewed attachment as the long-lasting connection developed between human beings. In discussing the nature of relationships, I pointed to our innate biological need to form bonds and seek connection. Bowlby, as well as other psychologists, have proposed that the drive to form attachments is something children are born with. Bowlby's ideas were further developed and expanded upon, particularly by fellow psychologist Mary Ainsworth. Ainsworth's research demonstrated the significant long-term impact of our early attachments.

From attachment theory, attachment styles have been identified, which psychologists and some coaches may use to help us understand our behaviour in our close or intimate relationships. Our behaviour patterns in relationships are described in four attachment styles, but some of the names given to these styles may vary.

Secure attachment is a positive form of attachment, which is optimal for healthy relationships. People with this attachment style tend to have good self-esteem and can have trusting long-term relationships. They tend to share their feelings with partners and friends while seeking support within their social network. The remaining three attachment styles tend to lead to dysfunction in relationships for a variety of reasons.

Avoidant attachment can be seen in children who do not seek much contact or comfort from their parents. As adults, such individuals often have problems with intimacy. They do not become emotionally invested in social or romantic relationships and are often unwilling to share their thoughts and feelings with others. These people often remain distant and prefer to rely on themselves rather than others.

If you find yourself reluctant to develop close romantic relationships while also feeling desperate to be loved by others, you may have a fearful-avoidant, also called disorganized attachment style. If you are in a relationship with someone whose feelings toward you seem to swing from anxious to avoidance, this may be their attachment style. It usually stems from those whose parents were a source of fear and reassurance.

Finally, signals of anxious attachment indicate a person who has a deep fear of abandonment. Such people tend to seek a lot of validation because they often worry their partner will leave them. This attachment style is prominent in those whose behaviour in relationships comes across as needy, and no matter the amount of reassurance they receive, it doesn't seem to be enough.

If you see any of these negative attachment styles in others, have compassion because it's likely that these people have not yet healed issues from their childhood. But also know that a relationship with them may be difficult unless they are willing to do the work to heal.

When you heal your traumas and other issues from your past, you can become more secure in your relationships. Changing your negative beliefs about yourself can also help by improving your self-esteem. In addition, learning to love yourself will significantly improve your sense of security in relationships. I used to have an unhealthy attachment style, but my positive philosophy and healing of my past helped me change this. Recognizing your attachment style may help you better understand your feelings and actions in relationships, as well as the beliefs that support them.

The relationship with you

In the earlier chapter, Self, I discussed ways to see yourself on different levels and from different perspectives. Since we are each a system rather than just one thing or one being, an automatic relationship forms between different parts of us. So, when I talk about your relationships with you, I am referring to the awareness, connection, and interaction between different elements of who you are. This can refer to the relationship between body and mind, mind and spirit, or you as an adult and your inner child. Ultimately, though, I am drawing attention to the present version of you and your interaction with the physical, mental, and spiritual aspects of you.

From a biological perspective, we experience the urge to pursue people our biology has programmed us to be attracted to. Traditionally, the male played the role of pursuer, leaving females to make themselves attractive and alluring to the opposite sex. A lot has changed, but we still have these biological impulses, and it helps to be aware of them because pursuing these impulses cannot only make us unhappy but get us into trouble. This is apparent in a man who is rejected by a woman but thinks he should try harder in his pursuit of her.

Our biology can cause us to be attracted to those who do not benefit us emotionally. The mental models we have developed can cause us to pursue partners who will lead us into dysfunctional relationships. Meanwhile, our intuitive or spiritual impulses could help guide us to relationships that nurture and fulfill us. Understanding our relationship to the different parts of who we are is essential to knowing ourselves and having quality relationships.

It sounds almost cliché to say that you cannot truly love another until you love yourself. Unfortunately, we do not tend to love ourselves unconditionally. There are parts of us we do not like and want to get rid of, but as I have already written, there is no getting rid of the parts that make us whole. If we can understand our needs and build a positive relationship with ourselves, we can begin to make progress. It is through better understanding ourselves that we can better learn to love ourselves.

Connection

"I believe that human connection has transformative power in all aspects of our lives."
- Esther Perel -

It is because I believe that connection is so critical to our health and happiness that I would like to close this chapter by sharing what I have learned from researcher, author, and inspiring storyteller Brené Brown. Brown emphasizes that connection is what gives purpose and meaning to our lives. More importantly, she has come to some important conclusions about what disrupts or undermines our connections with others.

Brené has identified shame as a key factor in undermining connection. In my philosophy, shame is fear-based, as with all negative emotions. In this case, Brown proposes that shame evokes a fear of disconnection. Shame leaves us feeling not good enough. In fact, our shame causes us to feel unworthy of connection.

Connection also requires vulnerability. In friendships, families, teams, and communities, the trust we need requires the willingness to tolerate some degree of vulnerability. A willingness to be vulnerable allows us to be truly authentic. This is difficult when we feel shame and unworthiness.

In her research, Brown has identified that people who are able to be vulnerable and authentic are able to connect with a sense of love and belonging. She refers to them as whole-hearted people. These people embrace vulnerability, but more importantly, they feel worthy of love and connection. This seems to be the key to deep, high-quality connections.

Why is vulnerability so difficult? Whether through conditioning or negative experiences, we slowly put up defences and begin to play different roles to meet the expectations of others. We become guarded and unsure of what makes us authentic. In Brown's view, we numb our vulnerability, but the issue is that we cannot just numb one feeling or emotion. Our emotional defences lead us to numb all our positive sensations, from joy and excitement to gratitude and happiness. In this way, Brown points out that we lose the sense of meaning we get from our connections. She leaves us with the following advice:

Let yourself be seen—as you are, mistakes and all.
Love with your whole heart, even without guarantees.
Practice gratitude and joy even when you're afraid.
Believe you are enough.

Conclusion

From the time we are born until we leave this world, most of us will come into contact with thousands of different people. Some contacts are brief, while others can last a lifetime. Some people we wish we had more time with, others we may wish we had never met. Many are quickly forgotten; some we cherish in our memories forever. Our interactions with each other, whether we consider them good or bad, are a critical part of our life's journey.

If you are to make sense of the joys and dramas that unfold as you mingle with all these people along life's path, then relationships deserve your attention as you develop your philosophy. What kind of people do you want in your life? How do you want to be treated and how will you treat others? What are your expectations? What do you want from the relationships that you have? These are all things that can be defined in your philosophy.

Before deciding on your answers to these questions, it may be necessary to take a good look at your current beliefs about relationships and discover what they mean to you. It goes beyond considering your relationships with friends, family, and all those close to you. From your relationship with one person to your relationship with the human race, what does this interaction mean to you on your journey of growth and experience?

Questions

- What do your relationships reflect about who you are and how you behave?
- What do your relationships trigger in you? Which emotions do they generate?
- Do you recognize strategies that you follow in your relationships? Do these strategies support happy and harmonious relationships?
- Think about the most prominent relationships in your life: family, work, friendships, romantic. How does each of these contribute to your happiness? How do you contribute or add value to these relationships?
- Do you recognize the different patterns of behaviour you exhibit in your various relationships? Do you understand what this behaviour is meant to help you achieve?
- What does your inner narrator say about your relationships?

12 COMMUNICATION

"The way we communicate with others and with ourselves ultimately determines the quality of our lives."
- Tony Robbins -

Our ability to share thoughts, feelings, and ideas through language is perhaps the greatest human achievement. It has allowed us to learn, grow, and share information through generations. The ability to communicate well is perhaps the most important factor for anyone seeking to succeed in the modern world. It is also the cornerstone of healthy and harmonious relationships.

In this chapter, I would like to explore how our beliefs and perceptions influence the way we communicate and the way we interpret communication. I will also try to raise awareness of what undermines good communication to help you develop new beliefs and strategies to help you communicate more successfully. When we feel understood and find ways to better understand others, we will lead happier lives.

Think of the joy and excitement we feel when someone really "gets" us or the connection we feel when we really understand each other. For almost fourteen years, I had a wonderful dog named Chloe. When she was young, I trained her to ring a bell at the front door when she needed to go out. She really got excited when I understood what she was trying to communicate to me, and this was not just limited to bell ringing. When young children are misunderstood, they can quickly become frustrated and cranky. The same can be true of many adults. In our relationships and interactions with others, our happiness is strongly correlated to our ability to be understood and relate to others. When we communicate well, it strengthens our sense of connection to others and supports our happiness.

Unfortunately, beyond essential reading and writing skills, most of us do not learn to communicate well. For the most part, we learn through imitation, and if we do not have good role models for communication, we are prone to inherit many bad habits. We also develop beliefs about how and what we should communicate and expectations relating to how others should respond or initiate communication with us.

Most communication is spontaneous, as most people do not often consciously rehearse or plan everyday conversations. I am not a communication expert, so I will not provide rules or guidelines to improve your communication. However, I do believe an elevated awareness of our beliefs, assumptions, and inner strategies will help us develop a philosophy which will lead to healthier and more productive interactions with each other.

The process of communication

"Between what I think, what I want to say, what I believe I say, what I say,
what you want to hear, what you believe to hear, what you hear,
what you want to understand, what you think you understand,
what you understand. . .there are ten possibilities that we
might have some problem communicating.
But let's try anyway. . ."
- Bernard Werber -

If you believe communication is a simple process, this might be the first assumption to address in your beliefs. On the surface, it may seem simple. We have an idea or something we want to express. We communicate this in words, and then one or more people receive our message. Of course, it is not that simple, and when the process does work, it is not a matter of simplicity but contributing factors that we are unaware of.

Let's look at the process more closely. In communication, there is a sender of information. This person encodes meaning into the message and shares or sends it to the receiver, who then decodes it. In other words, the receiver interprets the message and attempts to derive meaning from it. This usually leads to some form of feedback, whether it be a return message or body language. Even no response can be valuable feedback.

So much can interfere with the process being executed effectively. Both sender and receiver may have biases or assumptions about the other person or the message's meaning. Context, emotions, and distractions can also interfere with the process. Everything from the ambiguity of words to the different interpretations of a message can lead to misunderstandings or a false sense of agreement.

I have observed native English speakers talking to individuals who were not fluent in English. Some spoke quickly and with slang—even someone fluent might struggle to understand. We send messages encoded with meaning but may unknowingly deliver them in a way that they cannot be well-received or properly interpreted. Do you ever assume the other person is at fault when they do not understand you?

As we receive communication, we interpret or decode information. Our assumptions and biases influence how we interpret, and our emotions or current state will also play a role. Then our practiced or habitual responses may take over. In such cases, we may not be responding to current communication but to past situations or unresolved traumas. These are all factors to consider when reflecting on how well you communicate or how adept your listener or listeners are at receiving and understanding your message.

Whether you believe communication is difficult or easy, I hope that understanding the process in more detail has given you a better understanding of where things can go wrong. It is not nearly as straightforward as some may assume.

The problem with words

It is worth repeating here that words merely represent things, ideas, or feelings. Or, as Eckhart Tolle describes, words are pointers. They point toward what they are trying to describe. In this way, words can also be ambiguous because they are open to interpretation depending on their context.

In this book, I am attempting to explore very deep and complex subjects, and many words may be interpreted differently than I intended. I have encouraged you to be clear on your definitions of words for the philosophy you are trying to create, and it is important to remember that others may have slightly different interpretations or definitions of certain words. What are your words trying to point toward?

If you believe you know with certainty that your interpretations of words match perfectly with everyone else's, you will likely have frequent misunderstandings and conflicts. This is especially true if you assume you know the intentions behind the words you have interpreted. As a coach, I constantly clarify what other people's words mean. Sometimes this is for my own understanding, but other times it is to make sure the person I am coaching is fully aware of what they are saying.

As a writer, I love words and appreciate their value, but I have also come to recognize their limits. Some of the biggest challenges we face around communication are related to the words we use and the assumptions we make around their meaning and intention.

Non-verbal communication

Have you ever met someone for the first time or observed someone you didn't know and quickly sensed you liked or disliked them? Maybe you felt the need to judge them in some way based on how being in their presence made you feel. This may be an intuitive response because your unconscious has picked up on something you cannot rationally put your finger on. We all communicate things about ourselves, whether we are aware of it or not. A keen observer may pick up these non-verbal cues, but most people don't consciously perceive them. Where our conscious mind fails, our unconscious can be very perceptive. When it picks up a message, it communicates this to you through feeling. Thus, you have an intuitive response.

Most of our communication is non-verbal. Albert Mehrabian, a researcher of body language, observed face-to-face conversations and noted some interesting statistics. His research indicated that communication is 55 per cent non-verbal. However, although the remaining percentage was vocal, only 7 per cent was exclusively through the use of words. This has led some to claim that more than 90 per cent of communication is non-verbal. Regardless of the percentages, the majority of our communication is not only non-verbal but much of it is unconscious as well.

If you believe that the only things you are sharing with others are the words you consciously choose to share, you are mistaken. I have experienced people who were dishonest but got upset when someone didn't believe their lies. Or someone may have thought they said all the right things but still left a poor impression on someone they just met. These are all signs that your body language may be betraying you. That may be why the best liars find a way to believe their own lies. Hopefully, this knowledge will encourage you to communicate honestly with integrity and authenticity rather than trying to become a better liar.

The role of emotions in communication

You may recall from a previous chapter when I referred to feelings as communication and emotions as the reaction to those feelings. Again, this way of seeing this internal process helps me to guide and direct my emotions. This is especially relevant in communication.

When looking at the process of communication, one of the biggest causes of interference is emotions. The emotions that come from fear, anger, or distress will not only cause us to say and do things that are out of character for us, they can also distort the decoding of messages we hear from others. Naturally, this will lead to misunderstandings, but it can also lead us to develop inaccurate beliefs about those we interact with.

It is not only negative emotions that can distort our perspective. When we are feeling euphoric or filled with high levels of positive conviction driven by our emotions, the things we say may no longer ring true once the euphoria subsides. The things we say may not be authentic under such conditions, and we may pick out the positive things we want to hear in a conversation. These are times people profess their love to another because they are caught up in the moment, only to realize it was only their emotional state and not their authentic feelings.

Recognizing when positive or negative emotions are making it difficult to communicate effectively will help you in relationships and better understand yourself. In my philosophy, I try to speak out of love and listen with compassion. I do not always succeed, but this belief and way of approaching communication helps me continuously improve.

Our communication could be more effective if we took the emotion out. Our feelings are communication for us, not necessarily for other people. That is to say, our feelings provide guidance, but trying to translate this into words or explain this to another isn't always helpful. If someone gave you some tips, tricks, or insights to help you with a discussion or negotiation, would you use their input by saying, "So and so told me to say this…"? Or would you simply use the knowledge or understanding you had gained to guide your discussion?

Our emotions can signal passion, stress, or anger in ways that our words may not be able to. In this way, they have an important role. As part of your philosophy on communication, it is important to recognize and discern between the feelings that are guiding you and the emotions that are affecting your judgement. It is also important to learn when expressing emotion helps communication and when it interferes with the message you are trying to convey.

Dealing with conflict

Conflict can be a very healthy and productive element of communication. It is difficult to resolve issues, misunderstandings, and disagreements without healthy conflict. As Patrick Lencioni points out in his Five Dysfunctions model, without the willingness and ability to engage in healthy conflict, it will be difficult to find common ground and commit to common goals. The first step in dealing with conflict is then a willingness to talk openly about it.

The biggest challenge in trying to resolve conflicts is that we often try to approach them rationally. This may sound strange, but dealing with facts and observable details is not usually where the conflict lies between two people or two parties. On the surface, we may be talking about facts and recounting events, but what is below the surface are beliefs, assumptions, culture, attitudes, past experiences, and emotions. If you think of two people in conflict as icebergs, it is below the surface where they collide.

To create a long-term resolution of conflicts, it is essential to address what is below the surface. You cannot force the other party to do this, but you can start by looking at yourself and be willing to be vulnerable enough to share what is below the surface on your side. What beliefs do you have about the situation? Which assumptions have you made? What are your fears or expectations? And if you are really brave, what are you feeling?

What does all this tell you about communication in conflicts? Your beliefs guide what you think, feel, and say. They do this because they influence your perceptions and emotions. This is playing out in other people as well as yourself. If you start with the premise that the other person is the reason or cause for a conflict, you will struggle to resolve it. Looking at your own beliefs and assumptions will help you move forward.

Truth and honesty

In the nineties, I read a book by Gary Zukov called *The Seat of the Soul*. Back then, I wasn't sure if I even believed in a soul or, more importantly, what was meant by a soul, but I read it just the same. The statement from the book that Zukov makes that still resonates with me today is that the soul cannot stand being lied to. If I replace soul with inner being, higher self, or unconscious mind, this still rings true. There is a part of me, and perhaps in you, that feels a deep sense of hurt and betrayal when being lied to. Naturally, this can depend on the nature and gravity of the lie, but for the most part, people dislike being lied to.

As part of the process of developing a personal philosophy, I encourage people to define their own truth. In a world driven and structured more by belief than facts, truths are relative. Therefore, being honest is more about communicating what we believe is true.

Honesty is a value. For some, it is a core value, while for others, it is a matter of whether truth is convenient. I credit honesty and authenticity as the reasons for my success, both in business and as a coach. However, I haven't always been honest, even though I have always valued honesty. As with many people, fear has been the main trigger for moments when I was not completely honest. As I get older, I find being dishonest stressful, making life complicated and affecting how I feel about myself.

Those who believe in game theory may be very pragmatic with their relationship to the truth. For some, their willingness to be honest is a matter of who they are talking to or what they will gain by being dishonest. Perhaps there is a sense that honesty will lead to being taken advantage of or punished in some way. Many would be more inclined to be honest to the people close to them and who they trust while not giving a second thought to lying to a stranger.

Sometimes honesty takes courage, while other times, not being honest takes courage. If I had to tell a lie to save someone's life, it is highly likely I would. At this point in my life, I have embraced honesty as a core value and do my best not to let fear get in the way of living this value. This means there are very few circumstances where I would consciously lie. I am supported in this by my philosophy.

Much of our dishonesty stems from not being honest with ourselves. We convince ourselves of things we knew were not true at some point. Over time, in the same way one might use affirmations, we lie to ourselves to feel like we are being honest. A lie told enough times begins to feel like the truth.

Where does honesty rank in your values? If it is a core value but if you find yourself being dishonest regularly, you will feel this discontinuity. Your unconscious will let you know, and your self-image will be affected. In his role as Rob Roy in the movie of the same name, Liam Niesson says to his son, "Honour is a gift you give yourself." If you can find the courage to be honest, you can give yourself the gift of honour.

Non-violent Communication

No discussion about effective communication would be complete without mentioning the work of Marshall B. Rosenberg. Rosenberg was a psychologist who developed the concept of non-violent communication (NVC), which is helpful in both the workplace and personal relationships. Although I feel it is important to distinguish between physical violence and the harm that words can cause, the NVC approach to communication is very helpful in understanding the effect your words have, regardless of your intentions.

NVC focusses on your own needs and feelings in communication. In practice, this means you describe how a situation or message from another makes you feel and what your needs or preferences relating to a given situation are. This process recognizes that what you experience is based on your perceptions. What often happens, especially in conflict situations, is that people make accusations and place blame. This is often met with a defensive response, leading to exchanges that may not even deal with the issue at hand. As I pointed out in the section about dealing with conflict, we may communicate facts or rational arguments even though the issues are emotional and often go beyond words.

Far too often, when we give feedback, we tell people what they did or how they did it. We may accuse or blame people for their actions without fully understanding the situation beyond our interpretation of the events. This blaming and accusing is what Rosenberg refers to as violent communication because we go on the offensive or are verbally attacking someone.

What do you want others with whom you are communicating to understand? The NVC approach to communication could help you share your current experience with others more effectively and encourage them to do the same. In doing so, you may also learn to better understand your own intentions and strategies.

There are four areas or steps to consider in NVC. What can you observe? Try to avoid judgement and focus on actions and behaviours. Remember that what you perceive is an interpretation, and your inner narrator may have provided commentary and opinions that affect how you see things. Share how you feel. "When you do this, I feel like…" Focus on emotions that are being triggered. Then consider your needs. What do you need from the other person? Consider your needs and values. Finally, make a request. Be specific and clear about what you want. This is your chance to share your expectations.

Most people are not trying to provoke you to have a negative emotional response, so when you share how their words and actions make you feel, it creates more empathy and understanding. Letting people know how to better communicate with you or the effect their words and actions have upon you will help them adjust and improve if they are willing to do so. Especially those close to you, or people at work who want to have a good working relationship, will benefit from knowing how you feel. This kind of openness also creates more trust. Remember that a request does not state what the other should or must do. It asks if someone would or could interact with you in a particular way.

I want to reinforce my point that you cannot control the external world, including the people around you. You often cannot control your circumstances, but with the right tools, you can help guide your thoughts and feelings. The same is true when the words of another are hurtful and abusive. Although verbal abuse should not be tolerated, your exposure to it may be out of your control. You will have more success navigating communication and relationships if you develop the tools that give you more power to overcome the negative words that others direct at you. Rosenberg emphasized one important principle: you are responsible for how you feel.

Do you find yourself involved in a lot of conflicts or misunderstandings? Do you recognize how you contribute to these situations? If your beliefs and communication strategies are based on some form of game theory, you will struggle to find open, trusting, and honest communication with people. This will lead to disharmony and distance in your relationships. Hopefully, understanding the principles of non-violent communication will help you create beliefs around communication that will lead to more harmony and empathy in your relationships.

Listening

"Seek first to understand, then to be understood."
- Stephen Covey -

There is perhaps no more important skill in interactive communication than listening. The filter of our beliefs affects what we hear and the thoughts such perspectives generate. If you want to truly hear and understand what someone else is saying, it is important to find ways of suspending your judgement and keeping your biases in check. If you can approach listening with curiosity and empathy, your ability to hear well will be much better.

Much like communication, people seem to think listening is easy and natural, but it is a skill that needs to be developed. In a digital age of short attention spans, listening seems to be suffering more than ever. Since listening is perhaps the most important component of communication, I want to share some things to consider to help inform what you might think it means to listen well.

Perhaps the biggest obstacle to listening well is our mental chatter. As we try to listen, we are often distracted by the inner voices that judge, complain, and accuse. It may also be that we are thinking about ways to respond without listening fully to what another person has said. Add to this our ego, which often fuels the need to be right.

To listen well, we need to put ourselves into a state to listen. Whether we are trying to hear our inner voice or the voice of another, it is important to find calm and a distance from emotional chatter. From here, we can employ techniques related to non-violent communication. We can listen to the needs and values of the other person. We can try to sense what they are feeling, and we can look for a request; what are they asking of us?

If we learn to listen well, we will have better relationships, fewer misunderstandings, and more fulfilling conversations. Indeed, the world would be a better place with better listeners.

> *"Communication leads to community, that is, to understanding,*
> *intimacy, and mutual valuing."*
> - Rollo May -

Throughout this chapter, I have tried to stress the importance of communication to support success in work, relationships, and life in general. I have tried to point out that the ability to communicate well also increases your level of happiness. These ideas are meant to increase your awareness around the process of communication and the habits or assumptions you may have. Perhaps you can use these ideas to refine your beliefs around your perceptions, expectations, and strategies to communicate well. Once these are clear, practice is the key.

From my background in sales, management, and coaching, I have benefitted from a great deal of practice in improving my communication skills. These are the ideas that I have incorporated into my philosophy on communication. I do not always execute them perfectly, but the more I practice, the better I get. If you can improve the quality of your communication skills, your relationships will improve immeasurably.

Questions
- Do you consider yourself a good communicator? If so, what makes you good? If not, where would you like to improve?
- Do you have a strategy for communicating with others? Do you know which beliefs these strategies stem from? For example, do you believe that people are generally trustworthy, or are you careful

with how much you share about yourself?

- What do you value in communication? Honesty? Directness? Kindness? Compassion? Discretion? Cleverness?

13 LIFESTYLE

"The shoe that fits one person pinches another;
there is no recipe for living that suits all cases."
- Carl Jung -

Developing a personal philosophy is, in essence, a process of under-standing how to live well. Naturally, our beliefs and values drive our behaviour, but we can also develop specific beliefs about the routines and practices we want to live by. These beliefs can include everything from what to eat, when to sleep. and how to spend your time. These can be rules that you live by if that makes it easier for you to commit to them; however, you may prefer to see them as principles. Princi-ples allow you the freedom and agility to adapt to diverse situations and change.

Do you live a life that allows for your greatest happiness? Elon Musk believes you have to work like hell to succeed. Does working a sixty or eighty-hour work week allow for a happy life? If you love your work and it fulfills most of your needs, this might be possible. However, it is possible this type of philosophy toward work is missing some beliefs around health or emotional well-being. Those who seek a hedonistic, pleasure-focussed life may not have consid-ered a deeper meaning to life and developing a sense of purpose. Whether it is pleasure we seek or achievement in life, when our lifestyle is extreme or one-sided, there may be something critical that we are missing in how we live.

Which beliefs are behind the lifestyle that you live? It may be that you haven't really given it much thought. Your way of living may simply be an accumulation of habits you have fallen into. Or you may have some clear beliefs about one area of life while not giving much thought to another. In this chapter, I would like to encourage you to think about how you currently live and if one or more elements of your lifestyle could be negatively impacting your happiness. In doing so, I will ask you to consider the physical, mental, and spiritual conditions.

The physical

When considering my physical well-being, I focus on four areas in no particular order: eating and drinking, breathing, motion, and sleep. I have developed specific beliefs about how to optimize these for the best possible physical experience. As my knowledge grows through education or experimentation, my philosophy evolves accordingly. Although I strive to find ways to be happy independent of the conditions in my life, including health, having a healthy body will allow for more overall happiness.

Our knowledge and understanding of nutrition and the human body have grown immensely over the past decade or so. Along with a wide range of research has come a wide range of expert opinions on how to best feed our bodies. There are opinions on whether or not to eat meat, carbohydrates, sugar, and a number of other foods. There are debates around quantity and in what combination foods should be eaten, as well as when to eat. Experts may disagree, so it can be challenging for the average person to understand what is right for their body.

Many also seem to confuse the term diet with a period of time when we restrict our eating in some way. Often, this practice limits what and how much we eat. However, our diet is what we eat regularly or habitually and includes cultural or regional patterns of consumption. Instead of seeing a diet as something you go on for a period of time, it can be helpful to see yourself as having a specific diet. If we commit to a diet, by this definition, that is healthy, satisfying, and well-suited for our bodies, we would unlikely need to go on a diet to lose weight and feel better.

Two discoveries scientists have made about health in recent years are the importance of the microbiome and the impact of when or how often we eat. Our bodies consist of more bacteria cells than human cells, and what you feed your bacteria, particularly the bacteria in your gut, has huge implications on your overall health and immune system. The idea that we need three meals a day has also been challenged and, in fact, there may be significant benefits to being hungry for periods during the day or night. For example, I have found that limiting my meals to an eight-hour period every day has provided significant health benefits. There is a plethora of information to consider here, so I encourage anyone developing a philosophy on food not to overlook these two factors.

Eating is also a pleasure I enjoy and appreciate. When considering happiness, perhaps we can allow ourselves to go beyond the functional or practical. In my philosophy, eating is far more than just ingesting nutrients. Not everything I eat is healthy. I appreciate moments when I eat for pure enjoyment. I don't eat things that I do not enjoy. Even healthy food can be delicious. I know that alcohol has negative effects on the body, but I enjoy a glass of wine or a well-made beer on occasion. Although infrequently, I will even sip a well-made spirit from time to time. Quality and moderation are at the core of my philosophy around eating, and I believe that if we all took greater care to eat well, we would have far less need for doctors and medicine.

The liquid part of our consumption is also important. The body can go much longer without food than without water. More than two days without water can be fatal, but there are many other facts about dehydration that I find far more surprising. Did you know that your body can mistake your thirst for hunger? Sometimes when we feel hungry, it is actually our body telling us we are thirsty. Dehydration can cause everything from fatigue and tiredness to brain fog and even depression.

What we eat and drink is highly influenced by our culture and social norms within our family or community. The habits we form from these influences may not be the best for our health. What do your beliefs say about the food and drinks you consume? How important are they in living a happy life? If you said very important, is it because of the pleasure food brings you or the health it provides your body? In my philosophy, health comes before pleasure, but I do not underestimate how much our social connections and rituals around food also support our happiness.

Why do we breathe? The logical answer is to take in oxygen and release carbon dioxide. As with any complex system, the act of breathing has far greater implications than the inhalation and exhalation of gases. Perhaps the more important question is, "How do we breathe?"

Breathing is something we take for granted. It happens while we sleep, and even in our waking hours, we barely take a moment to notice our breathing. How we breathe is far more important than most people realize. Improving how you breathe can positively impact your stress level, blood pressure, quality of sleep, and overall health.

In his book *Breath: The New Science of a Lost Art*, journalist James Nestor explores scientific research around breathing and breathing techniques from various cultures in history. Nestor documents how most people breathe in a way that is detrimental to their health. Ten years of learning breathing practices and investigating research led to two significant conclusions. It is best to breathe through your nose, and the optimal breath consists of a five-and-a-half-second inhale and exhale for the same duration.

From practicing yoga and meditation, I have learned a number of different breathing methods. I use them to create inner calm and help focus my mind. Several years ago, I also learned the Wim Hof breathing method, which I suspect is rooted in ancient yogic methods. However, the Wim Hof method provides additional health benefits, including helping my body fight off oncoming cold or flu symptoms. The ability of my breath to heal or fight off illness may just be my perception, but the Wim Hof method is being studied and does indeed seem to have many positive health benefits.

Why is knowledge about breathing important for our philosophy? Part of the process of developing a philosophy is to raise awareness around our beliefs, thoughts, and the processes of life. If you can calm your mind and improve your health by just breathing, it is something worth noting in your philosophy.

If you know someone committed to a healthy lifestyle, they will likely have a regular exercise regime. Keeping your body in motion benefits the whole body, including the brain. Regular exercise has many benefits, but how to exercise varies greatly. I do not have a rigorous exercise program. I play basketball regularly and I practice yoga, but I do not enjoy going to a fitness club. I also walk or cycle daily. I am not a high-level athlete, but I feel healthy, and my body still responds well to exercise. My techniques work well for me, but they may not for you.

If you don't enjoy exercise, do you know why? Our bodies are made to move, and without movement, our health will suffer. If you don't enjoy some kind of movement, maybe you haven't tried the right activities, or maybe it is time to review your beliefs and mental models around exercise.

Finally, ideas around sleep have changed and evolved over the years. I remember reading more than twenty years ago that, according to science, there was no clear reason why the human body needs sleep. We now know that sleep is essential, and a lack of it can cause numerous health issues. Poor or insufficient sleep can cause cardio-vascular issues, mood disorders, obesity, stress, and many other physical issues common in society today. Both quality and quantity of sleep are important to reflect on when determining what is best for your body.

Among the important details to include in your beliefs around sleep is that there is a difference between the ability to fall asleep and the quality of sleep. People who take sedatives to fall asleep or feel they can sleep better after consuming alcohol should know that although this may help you enter sleep, the quality of your sleep can be negatively affected. Marijuana is also used by some for relaxation, but it can inhibit REM sleep. For regular users of this drug, the quality of sleep can be significantly impacted.

Fortunately, I rarely have trouble sleeping, so I used to take it for granted. Now that I've been made aware of the importance of sleep, I have recognized that although I fall asleep easily most of the time, the quality of my sleep has not always been optimal. Neurobiologist Andrew Hubermann from Stanford University points out that sleep is the best stress relief, trauma release, immune booster, hormone augmentation, and emotional stabilizer. He also provides some excellent tips for improving your sleep. These include: going outside within thirty to sixty minutes of waking to take in natural light (and doing the same just before dusk), waking up at the same time every day, avoiding caffeine eight to ten hours before sleep, avoiding bright lights after 10 p.m., and his list continues. People with sleep disorders may need to take stronger measures.

Sleeping patterns change with age, so it is important to update your beliefs on sleep as you get older. Over half of people in most Western countries experience difficulty falling asleep, sleep duration, or sleep quality. When you look into the science, your beliefs around sleep may change, along with your awareness of how your lifestyle affects your sleep.

Again, these are the four areas I have found most strongly affect the quality of my physical experience: eating and drinking, breathing, exercise, and sleep. You may have specific health issues that cause you to focus more on one or another area altogether. There are other habits that affect multiple areas of health. For example, I take cold showers for the positive effects on my immune system, quality of sleep, and other positive physical effects. You don't need to have the perfect lifestyle to live well, but focussing on a few areas that have the greatest impact on your health and well-being will lead to greater happiness.

The mental

My philosophy around mental well-being has helped me identify habits and tools that support my mental health and resilience. I am inclined to say that addressing this area of my life and finding the lifestyle that best improved my mental experience made the biggest impact. However, everything is interrelated. It is difficult to separate body, mind, and spirit. Nonetheless, I would like to explore some lifestyle choices that impact our mental experience.

When I refer to lifestyle choices with regard to our mental experience, I am pointing to the kind of environment and external input that we expose ourselves to, as well as the mental habits we cultivate. There are people and experiences that we repeatedly expose ourselves to that have a negative impact on our psyche. The same is true of the thoughts we allow ourselves to continue thinking without question. Good mental health requires good habits and discernment around what we expose our minds to.

In my mid-thirties, I radically changed my life. I left my life in Canada and started my new life by travelling through Asia for six months. During this time, I had little or no exposure to the news. It was the longest I had ever gone without watching TV. It is difficult to say that this alone contributed to my positive state of mind since I was not working and enjoying travel in new and interesting countries. However, once settling in Europe, I continued to avoid exposure to the news. With the onset of digital media, avoiding the news became more difficult, and with my interest in certain issues in the news, my resistance to exposure waned. As I reflect on this change, I perceive a correlation between the amount of news I watch and my levels of positivity and optimism. What has also helped me is to balance bad news with good news. I try to listen to talks and inspiring stories of people finding solutions and making a positive impact on the world.

When we inundate ourselves with information telling us how bad the world or our environment is, what does that do to us? Does it motivate us to positive action? Or does it cause a fear response? How does our view of the world inform our beliefs and actions? What role are we inclined to play in the world if it is a dangerous unforgiving place? I will leave it up to you to make the cost and benefit calculations of being informed. However, I would point out that there is a difference between being informed and completely immersing yourself in the world of modern media.

There seems to be a strong correlation between nature and mental well-being. Unfortunately, modern city living often keeps us indoors and, these days, virtually connected with the world. How much daily exposure do you give yourself to nature, or even just being outside in daylight? What are your beliefs about your connection to nature?

Another element of your lifestyle and environment is the company you keep. What kinds of people do you surround yourself with? Are these loving, supportive people? Are the attitudes of the people you engage with negative and cynical or positive and optimistic? Do people around you complain a lot? I avoid places where there is a lot of negativity and complaining. I will pay more to shop where people are friendly, both staff and other shoppers. Naturally, this is a luxury not everyone has, but when you have the choice or opportunity to interact with people who are friendly and positive, it is worth it. I also don't want this to sound elitist. Stores where wealthy people shop can be unfriendly and pretentious. Being poor or financially well off does not necessarily determine how you interact with the world. I have encountered some of the friendliest people in the world in some of the poorest places.

These are just a few examples to create awareness around the contribution that people and other external stimuli make to your mental state. Authentic happiness cannot be reliant on the external world to fit our needs and expectations, but when we have a choice, we can make decisions that support greater happiness. Some of these choices are also about our habits and behaviours.

Many of us live busy lives. I have coached people in business to help them with their time management. So often, I hear the phrase, "I don't have enough time!" I point out that we all have the same amount of time each day. Each of us has twenty-four hours every day, and we can choose how to fill this time. We prioritize things, both consciously and unconsciously. A lifestyle of good mental health may require us to reprioritize how we spend our time.

What don't you have time for? Exercise? Meditation? Sleep? What do you take time for? Work? Binge-watching movies and shows? Making time for practices that support a positive mental state is a habit that will contribute to less stress, more ease, and greater happiness. These are things such as meditation, time in nature, and nurturing positive and loving relationships. In the last chapter, I will share some practices to help contribute to a lifestyle that supports a positive mental experience.

The spiritual
Cultivating a lifestyle that supports our spiritual experience does not require regular visits to a church or temple. Many lifestyle choices

that support our mental experience also help on a spiritual level, except that this goes deeper and is more difficult to describe in words. It has nothing to do with your rational thinking mind but far more with your inner being. What is your relationship with yourself, and what is your unconscious trying to tell you?

The spiritual beliefs that I live by allow me to gain a sense of purpose and a better understanding of my feelings and emotions. This is where my beliefs around consciousness come into play. Whether you believe your consciousness is limited to the confines of your brain or expands beyond it, there is still an unconscious part of you that has needs and expresses them in feelings and impulses. The relevant question is then, is your lifestyle in alignment with your innermost needs and desires?

An important step in getting to know and understand your spiritual and emotional self is to get clear on your values. Values are not things we generally choose but things we resonate with. They reflect our deepest needs and desires, such as freedom, honesty, integrity, ambition, and authenticity. When we live according to our values, we are often aligned with our spiritual needs. Unfortunately, we sometimes sacrifice our values for money, success, or as a result of our fears. Living according to our values will better help us find meaning and purpose.

The unconscious part of us that I refer to as the spiritual self is often sending us signals and messages. As I have already shared early in the book, this is what I refer to as intuition. It is these signals that we need to listen to in order to better understand our spiritual experience. If we practice and learn to trust our inner signals and recognize the difference between them and our emotional triggers and fear responses, we will develop a deep connection to this part of us. This will help us to better look within.

It is especially on a spiritual level that we need a sense of connection and community with others. In my view, creating deep, meaningful connections and feeling a sense of belonging are spiritual needs. To this point, I have not connected the experience of the spiritual self with religion or spirituality. It is through such belief systems and organizations that some can develop communities and find a sense of connection. This can also be done by connecting with any group of people who share similar values.

I used to think this kind of spiritual stuff was just a lot of woo-woo and wishful thinking. My beliefs kept me from developing a lifestyle that allowed for spiritual growth. I used to think psychotherapy was for crazy people and prayer was for the gullible. Prayer is not my approach to spirituality, but meditation certainly is, and the two are not as far apart as I once thought. What do you believe about therapy? Are you open to exploring your emotional needs or even the pain you may have buried under layers of your personality? A lifestyle that makes room for spiritual development will lead to greater happiness.

All three levels of experience are interconnected and thus influence each other. Within our systems, the body, mind, and spirit all influence and affect one another. Healing is often a combination of all three. It is possible to heal physical symptoms temporarily, but the mental and spiritual traumas of our past will keep illness coming back if we don't resolve them.

I have shared many ideas for you to consider. Perhaps they have intrigued you enough to explore them further and to find more content for your personal philosophy. Hopefully, these ideas will help you create a lifestyle for sustainable health and happiness.

Questions

Is the way you are currently living contributing to your happiness? If not,

- What area of your life would you most like to change?
- What do you need more of and what do you need less of?

- Do you feel you have the power to change?
- What resources do you need to create a lifestyle that would allow you to live a happier, healthier life?

14 PASSING

"Life and death are one thread, the same line viewed from different sides."
- Lao Tzu -

Regardless of your spiritual beliefs, what you believe about death has a significant impact on the way you live your life. Even if you are not consciously thinking about death regularly, and hopefully you are not, beliefs around the subject can impact your choices and how you treat others. Such beliefs impact the risks we take and the habits we develop. These beliefs may change over time and certainly by the time we reach the end of our lives. In this chapter, I will encourage you to consider your beliefs about what the end of physical life means to you.

Our beliefs about who we are and what consciousness is play a key role when considering what death means. Is consciousness an emergent property of the physical brain? If energy cannot be created or destroyed, as Einstein proposed, what form could the energy that drives our physical existence take when the body dies? Do we have a soul? Can you imagine not existing? Your answers to questions like these point to whether you believe life is limited to this physical existence or if it continues in some other form when the body dies. No one can tell you the answers to these questions with any certainty, but it is important that you come to some conclusions about the nature of death.

Perhaps choosing what to believe about the nature of death seems binary. Either you believe there is life after death or you don't. I suppose for people who believe we have one life to live and there is nothing else, it may seem pretty black and white. We can choose to be agnostic on the subject and admit there is no way to know for sure. If we do believe in an afterlife, what does that look like? Do you believe in reincarnation? Do you believe in heaven and hell? No matter what you believe, the question is, how does this belief impact the way you live?

The way we approach death differs from culture to culture. Every culture has some ritual associated with death; in the West, we seem to sanitize it. We take brief moments to honour and remember the dead, but we don't want to be confronted with the process of leaving this world. We are entertained by violence and death in a way that can be foreign and unemotional, numbing us to reality. In poor or war-torn countries, death is far more real and present in people's lives. In such conditions, it is difficult to look away and ignore the inevitability of physical death.

An awareness of the finite nature of this life has many benefits. It can help us live more in the present and take action in the now rather than putting things off. This is not a call to encourage the fear of death to motivate us. We often use a greater fear to help us move past a lesser fear. This may work for some, but fear will never lead us to where we want to go. If we allow our vision of the future and the satisfaction of who we are to pull us toward achievements and the life we want, we will be motivated without the cloud of fear hanging over us. We will avoid the poor decisions made out of fear.

The fear of death

Perhaps it is because I have contemplated death for so long and imagined many possible ways of ending my life that I do not fear death. I do, however, have an irrational fear of heights. Is this not also a fear of death? While I am not afraid of being dead, there are plenty of ways I would not like to die. I have some fears about how I die, but not of death itself. Another fear is being badly injured but still alive. The idea of being in a coma on life-support and completely dependent on others for the most basic daily functions is a life I consider unbearable.

Again, it is not the fear itself but the beliefs, thoughts, and behaviours that result from such fears that matter. Our response to fear is what matters most. This is not a recommendation to live recklessly and throw caution to the wind. Self-preservation is something I strongly encourage. Remember, courage is not the absence of fear but the ability to act despite our fears, which seems to be a variation of a similar quote from Franklin D. Roosevelt. I am trying to point out that there is a difference between being courageous and being reckless.

I once knew a nurse who worked in the cancer ward of the Vancouver Children's Hospital. She told me that the most courageous ones in the hospital were the children who were terminally ill. According to her, it was often the kids who were giving emotional support to their parents and other family members. When we come to terms with death and no longer fear it, perhaps a kind of liberation follows.

Can you recognize the fear of death in any of your choices, thoughts, or behaviours? In a crisis such as a pandemic or a natural disaster, the way we act toward each other will be impacted by the degree to which we fear death and our strategy for dealing with this fear. Some will seek allies or a group to support each other. Some believe it is everyone for themselves and thus act selfishly, often following game theoretic strategies. Then there are some who are willing to sacrifice themselves for the sake of others.

What about everyday life? What kinds of choices do you make that may in some way be influenced by your fear of death or attempts to ignore it? Fear of death is woven throughout many people's personal beliefs.

Quality of life

One thing that considering death more closely will often trigger is taking stock of the life we are currently living. For those who have lost someone close to them or have faced a risk of dying but survived, it is not uncommon to reconsider how they live and the quality of their lives.

When I sometimes observe people being swept along by the river of life without reflection or immersed in illusions, I question whether we are all equally alive. Having now lived more than half of my life, I am no longer drawn to the things I used to strive for. It is not that I carry many regrets because my journey has led me to my current awareness, and without this experience, I would not have the understanding that I do. It is an understanding of what increases the quality of my life.

I am ambitious and willing to work hard. The question I now ask is, to what end and at what cost? *Walden* is a philosophical book that has inspired many. In it, Henry David Thoreau writes, "The cost of a thing is the amount of what I will call life which is required to be exchanged for it, immediately or in the long run." Is what you are exchanging your life for worth the price you are paying?

When I hear young people aspiring to be a YouTube sensation or the winner of some television talent contest, it reminds me of my teenage dreams of being a rock star. My dreams back then were driven far less by a passion for music than by a deeper need to be acknowledged, accepted, and loved. I had beliefs of being unworthy and unlovable, leading me to pursue not a fulfilling life but one that would soothe my fears. Much of what I tried to accomplish did not consider the quality of the life I wanted to live.

As we chase dreams and desires influenced by fear-based beliefs, we may sacrifice the happiness, love, and intangible qualities life offers us. With this in mind, it is important to ask ourselves what the success, possessions, and experiences we are pursuing are meant to fulfill. What does it mean to live a quality life?

Finite or infinite?

Throughout this book, I have asked questions that may have helped you consider more closely who you are. Who are you in part or in whole? Who are you in relationships? Who are you in thoughts, in your mind? This section title is another such question, and to explore it further, I will be considering the physical, mental, and spiritual perspectives.

The easiest level of experience to clarify is the physical. Clearly, the physical is finite. We develop in our mother's womb. We are born, and after some time, our bodies shift from growth to decline. Eventually, our physical bodies deteriorate or become diseased to the point that they can no longer support life. We can observe this and see that a lifeless body decays and becomes one with the physical world again.

From the mental perspective, it is not as clear. Is it definite that we no longer experience thoughts of any kind when our physical experience ends? If you believe that consciousness is an emergent property of the brain, then this would make sense. If consciousness extends beyond the physical limits, then there is more to consider. Using the internet as a metaphor, when we shut down a computer, a server, or even a hub, the internet continues. If we are part of a network of consciousness, do our thoughts and some version of who we are continue in the collective when our brain permanently shuts down? Perhaps not in the way we were expressed in physical form, but it may be that our legacy lives on in fragmented form in the memories and consciousness of others. Or could it be that a distinct version of ourselves remains active in the ether of some universal consciousness?

The spiritual perspective is one that I did not think was worth considering for many years. My assumptions about the meaning of a spiritual experience had me believing this was the realm of religion and superstition, and I did not make much of a distinction between the two. To this point, I have discussed the spiritual perspective in terms of our unconscious or emotional experience. Adding a dimension of energy to our definition of the spiritual can give us another perspective.

Over the years, I have returned to Einstein's assertion that energy cannot be created or destroyed. It can only change form. If we consider that, at a fundamental level, everything is energy, perhaps it is possible that our energy simply changes form when we are no longer attached to the physical. Could it be that the soul or the higher self are just names we give to energetic versions of ourselves which transcend the physical? Naturally, this is impossible to prove with our current abilities and levels of awareness. As with most things in life, the choice is yours as to what you believe.

As you may have noticed, my beliefs on this topic are not that clearly defined, but I have defined them enough to guide my philosophy. There are some things I cannot believe with complete clarity because they are likely beyond my brain's ability to conceive of them. Again, what matters here is: How does your belief around this question impact your life? Do you live this life in expectation of an afterlife? Do you believe there is only one life to live? Either way, these beliefs will impact how you choose to live your life.

There are plenty of ways to look at how we, or at least our consciousness, could exist beyond the physical brain. I have only covered a few here, and even a great scientific mind such as Sir Roger Penrose believes that consciousness is not a computation, such as would be performed in a computer. However, when defining your beliefs, I encourage you to consider the scientific view that consciousness is limited to the brain. Dr. Demis Hassabis, for example, disagrees with Penrose. Hassabis is a British artificial intelligence researcher who also studied neuroscience as part of his PhD and has concluded that there is no evidence of a quantum component needed for consciousness in the brain and that it can all be explained by classical theories of mind.

"The cradle rocks above an abyss, and common sense tells us that our existence is but a brief crack of light between two eternities of darkness."
- Vladimir Nabokov -

Most biologists and neuroscientists that I am aware of do not seem to believe that consciousness is infinite. Anyone with a spiritual perspective tends to believe there is an infinite element to who and what we are. Which belief serves your greatest happiness? Or is there another entirely different way to look at this question?

Grief

Loss is part of life. For some, the loss of someone they feel a close connection to and love dearly can impact their entire life. Experiences such as losing a parent at a young age, a parent losing a child, or someone losing a life partner prematurely can have lasting effects on our happiness. How we make sense of death in such situations can impact our happiness for years or even a lifetime. Our beliefs around death play an important role here. If you have lost someone close to you, how did you deal with it? How did you grieve? Did your beliefs around death have an impact on this experience?

What does it mean to grieve? It's important to remember that grief may feel like depression, but it is distinctly different from a mental and physical process. It is also not just the sense of sadness we associate with loss. It is also a sense of yearning and desire for something out of reach. Our philosophy around death can help us let go and relieve the yearning for the connection to someone we have lost.

There are many social norms and traditions associated with the death of a loved one or someone from a community. How should one act when confronted with such a death? Do you believe you need to be strong and work through your feelings alone? Should you express your grief outwardly so that everyone recognizes your pain? How long should you grieve? If you are considering what others think of your grieving processes, your focus is misplaced and unhelpful because there is no one right way in the grieving process.

Each of us has our way of grieving, and how we go through the process depends on our mental state or phase of life at the time and the support we have around us. Swiss-born psychiatrist Elisabeth Kuebler-Ross was a pioneer in helping people go through the process of losing a loved one. Together with David Kessler, she wrote a book about the *Five Stages of Grief.* The five stages are denial, anger, bargaining, depression, and acceptance, but these steps are often misunderstood. These stages are not necessarily experienced in a particular order, and not everyone goes through each stage. It is therefore not a five-step program for grief but rather a way to reflect and understand what our needs might be at any given stage of our grieving process.

David Kessler tells us that the five stages are not a road map to guide us through our grief. Each of us experiences grief in our unique way—grief will vary from person to person. My dog Chloe was a faithful companion I raised from a puppy when she was only eight weeks old. When she died a month before her fourteenth birthday, it was a far more intense grieving process than I expected. I found myself qualifying my grief by saying things like, "I know she was just a dog but..." Some belief in me said I wasn't allowed to grieve for an animal the way we grieve for the loss of a person. There are no such rules for grief.

Grief is not just a mental or spiritual process. It is also a physical process, and there is new research that helps us understand the neuroscience of grief. Science does not distinguish physical, mental, and spiritual since the assumption is that all of our experiences stem from the physical processes in the brain and body. At least this is all that can be objectively studied by science.

Prof. Andrew Huberman, from Stanford University in California, refers to several studies that help us understand the biology and neuroscience of grief. It is through his summary of the research that I have gained a better understanding of the physical experience of grieving.

Our psychological and physical state when we are confronted with grief strongly indicates the severity of our grief. Huberman points out that people can experience complicated and uncomplicated grief, with the first being a very prolonged period of bereavement which in many cases requires some form of mental health support. Roughly one in every ten people who experience grief suffer from the complicated variety.

Our depth of connection or attachment to another person will significantly influence the intensity and duration of our grief. Someone might lose a parent with whom they did not have a close, healthy relationship, and therefore not grieve as deeply as for a close friend, for example.

There are a number of interesting points that Huberman shares to help us better define and understand grief. First, it is both a state of pain and a state of wanting. Science actually refers to grief as a motivational process. This has been demonstrated by brain scans of people experiencing grief, in which the areas of the brain associated with motivation, craving, and pursuit are activated. Dopamine, which is commonly associated with pleasure and reward, during grief triggers a craving for the one we have lost. In grief, we enter an anticipatory state where we are waiting for something to happen. This can lead us to want to take action to resolve our craving, even though there is nothing we can do to actually fulfill that craving.

Dimensions are what scientists use to describe an aspect of the external world represented in the brain. Huberman explains that there are three dimensions that the brain uses to map out our relationships with people and things. The first is space, in terms of how far away we are from the person we have a relationship with. The second is time, as in the amount of time we require to physically meet, and finally, the third is closeness or the depth/intensity of our attachment to them.

When I apply these dimensions to my own life, I recognize how they reflect my sense of connection with people. Some people live an hour away by car from me who I do not see as much as someone who is an hour's plane ride away. The space between us is more, but the travel time is the same. Since I no longer own a car but still travel for work, this can play a role. Then when I consider that my brother lives in Canada, which is more than ten hours away by plane, the closeness of our relationship clearly outweighs the other two factors.

When someone passes away, we may still expect to see them or have trouble disconnecting their presence in a particular place. After my dog died, I would still expect to see her coming to greet me when I came home. There would be a split second where I would think, "Where is Chloe?" Why are these three dimensions important? To help overcome grief, Huberman explains, we need to remap our mental connection to these people.

Is our inability to reconcile the physical world, which we understand logically, and the emotional world, where our relationships are anchored, a sign of dysfunction in the mind? Or could it be confirmation that our physical, mental, and spiritual experiences are distinct from one another despite their reliance on each other? Our brain can have difficulty processing that someone or something from our experience is no longer with us. It has even more difficulty imagining ourselves no longer present in the world. Is this just an error in the brain, or is there a deeper reason many perceive themselves as more than just their physical bodies on some level of awareness?

It can be difficult to decouple someone you have lost from the time and space you associate them with. An approach I found helpful was a visualization process. When I get into a meditative state, I sometimes visualize an image of my grandmother who passed away in the late 1980s. When my dog died, I started to see her in this same visualization alongside my grandmother. This helped me associate a different time and space for my dog from the places in my house where I used to see her.

Rituals can also be a helpful way to process grief and loss. I never really understood the rituals and ceremonies that people participate in after someone has passed away. Surprisingly, it was when my dog died that I found peace through creating my own ritual. The company I had hired to dispose of my dog's remains offered to send me her ashes. I was going to decline but decided to take them up on their offer at the last minute. Once I received Chloe's ashes, I walked through the park area behind my house, along the path we so often walked together. When I found a place that felt right, I spread her ashes amongst the trees and plants where she used to explore. This ritual helped me make a mental shift so I could let go of the physical connection to my dog while still cherishing her memory.

The nature of death can be a challenging one to contemplate and even more difficult to define for your personal philosophy. Whatever you decide to believe, it is important to consider the effect this part of your philosophy has on your choices and the way you live your life. From the grief that you will inevitably feel during moments of your life to the fear of death that may loom over you from time to time, these can deeply affect your ability to be happy. In this realm of the unknowable, your beliefs can be a comfort and a guide.

Questions
- What do you believe about death?
- Does this belief influence how you live your life?
- Can you notice choices and behaviours that you have that are driven by this belief?
- Do your beliefs about living and dying help you come to terms with the loss of others and your own mortality?

15 PRACTICE AND PATIENCE

"For the things we have to learn before we can do them, we learn by doing them."
- Aristotle -

New beliefs not practiced will fade quickly. Beliefs worn like a badge or flown like a banner to convince the world of something will have little impact on inner systems and behaviours. Even deeply held beliefs around religion or politics may have a limited effect if they are not lived. Creating a practice around your beliefs will help you live them. It is the combination of defining the beliefs that support you and then turning them into practices that will create the life you desire. More moments of happiness will result.

You can spend your whole life trying to mentally understand philosophical ideas, but philosophy cannot fully be understood through contemplation or rational thinking. Only through practice can we fully understand its impact on our lives.

We cultivate practices in our lives not because we will one day arrive at a particular result. Instead, we actively pursue such behaviours because the practice of them makes our life better. It is the small things we do regularly that make the most difference in our lives. We become what we practice.

Many years ago, while getting certified as a basketball coach, I came across the term "sophomore syndrome." It refers to the slump that many athletes fall into during their second year of college. The slump was due to a sense of slowed progress or, in some cases, athletes felt they got worse from their first year. In reality, the learning curve in the first year of college is so steep, and then improvement so great, that it can seem to some as if they had stagnated or were getting worse in their second year. If you make a 100 per cent improvement in one year, it will be difficult to double your knowledge and ability again in the second year. When comparing to previous growth, your improvement of 20 per cent may seem like stagnation, or if you're really hard on yourself, you may perceive regression.

Sophomore syndrome can affect us in all areas of life, from professional sports to a new job or hobby. There is a competency continuum where we go from novice to competent to experienced and then to mastery and expertise. If we compare our rate of improvement from novice to competent as we work our way to mastery, it can be discouraging.

When I first started going to therapy, exploring philosophy and reconsidering my spiritual beliefs, the changes in my life felt like giant leaps forward. As the years passed, I got discouraged and frustrated and thought I had regressed. Perhaps my deficits were just too entrenched for me to change. When I look back now at my evolution since that first year or so of change, I have come a long way. Change takes time and requires patience. Patience is not complacency or procrastination. It is a continued effort, and persistence matters even when it feels like you are going one step forward and two steps back. Patience is the trust that the results you want will come if you practice the right things. Don't judge your progress in moments of weakness or failure. Have faith and trust that when practicing and correcting, you will improve.

In this chapter, I would like to focus on two things: prioritizing and integrating practices into daily life and reflecting and measuring progress to allow for patience and optimism. Patience and practice are the two most fundamental components of living your philosophy, creating more moments of happiness in your life, and maintaining a fulfilling level of growth and learning.

Interfering beliefs

Plenty of beliefs keep us from starting or maintaining a practice, just as there are numerous beliefs that cause us to lose patience and give up. Throughout this book, I have encouraged you to reflect on your beliefs based on their utility in your life. The same applies here. Now you can start to apply what you have learned in previous chapters. Do you remember how you change beliefs and patterns of thinking?

Hopeless thoughts and beliefs may surface soon after you begin a new practice. I look at it the same way as when discussing food and nutrition. A practice is not going on a diet; it is having a diet. This diet consists of the daily behaviours you want to have in your life. For this, we need to check our beliefs related to our expectations. Lasting change comes from small changes practiced over time. It is like compounding interest. If we look for reasons things aren't working out, we will find them.

Our past experiences around attempts at change can also support unhelpful beliefs. It is important to remember that you are not the person you were then. You are a new version of yourself. The only lessons you need from the past are what worked and what didn't. This can tell you what to do again or what not to do again. Any beliefs that say you are not good at something or can't do something are part of a fixed mindset that will stand in the way of maintaining a practice.

Hope is a term that has been both encouraged and discouraged. The kind of beliefs that I encourage are hopeful, optimistic beliefs about opportunities. I do not pursue the kind of hope that gives responsibility for choices and actions that concern me to others. The kind of hope that leads to complacency, procrastination, or helplessness keeps us waiting for external events to align before we can move forward.

Routines

Everything in this book can be practiced and requires practice to create habits and improve proficiency. A great way to develop a practice is to integrate it into a daily routine. Everyone, from highly successful people to highly spiritual people (of course, the two are not mutually exclusive), has routines to start their day, end their day, or follow at particular points in the day. We all have morning or evening routines, such as brushing our teeth or showering. These are habits we perform automatically every day.

If your morning routine includes drinking coffee and watching or reading the news, ask yourself if this is the best way to start your day. Consider the conclusions you came to in the Lifestyle chapter. Things I like to do in the morning include yoga and meditation, a cold shower, drinking water, and exposure to natural light and nature. Since I travel a lot and my mornings may start at different times in different time zones, I have variations of what I do, but doing them every morning is the key. For most people with a regular schedule, doing the same things daily is ideal for developing habits.

Highly effective people may have routines they engage in at any point throughout the day. Some people will take a power nap for ten minutes, while others will do a quick workout. Taking focus time or breaks from the demands of a busy day increases productivity and reduce stress. There are any number of mindfulness exercises that can become part of a midday routine. Think back to the chapter on the Present and the advice of Thích Nhất Hạnh.

Evening routines can help us destress and release the activities and experiences of the day to allow for a clear mind and better sleep. Although I prefer to meditate in the morning, for some, an evening meditation is the perfect way to end the day. Evenings are also a great time for reflection as long as you don't get lost in the details and start ruminating on them. For those who are religious, evening prayer can be a powerful and calming ritual. Even a simple ritual such as reading every night before bed can, depending on the content, clear the mind and disconnect from the events of your day. One of the most powerful evening rituals I enjoy focusses on gratitude. You may write a gratitude journal or make a mental list of the things you are most grateful for. Anything that prepares you for sleep and primes you for a good start in the morning can be turned into a daily evening routine.

If you're unsure where to start in terms of developing the right routines for you, it might help to consider your needs based on the physical, mental, and spiritual. What does my body need? Is it rest, stretching, exercise, or a nutritional boost? What does my mind need? Do I need to calm my busy mind or do I seek that creative spark? What are my emotional needs? What does my intuition say about the wants and needs of my unconscious?

Another way to decide which routines would benefit you the most in the present is to consider the behaviours you want to change. I hear the advice given frequently: Do something every day that scares you. If your inner critic is strong or you suffer from excessive internal chatter, your daily routine can include positive affirmations. Regardless of what you practice daily, make sure you believe in its utility and find enjoyment in it. Try to measure your progress. These will help you stay motivated until the habit is entrenched. And, as Mihaly Csikszentmihalyi explains, finding enjoyment in your tasks will help you enter a flow state.

Priorities

The most common reason people give for not being able to commit to certain practices in their lives is that they don't have time. I don't doubt that many people have very full lives with many commitments and obligations. We all have twenty-four hours in a day. We cannot earn more or buy more time. The only thing we can do is choose what we will spend our time on. We all have things we know would make us feel better if we did them regularly. The questions are: Do you want to? Can you? And will you? Instead of saying you don't have time, maybe try admitting it just isn't a priority.

Over the years, I have learned a long list of really helpful activities to practice. So many, in fact, that I could fill each day with one helpful practice after another. Since I have a lot of other things I want to achieve, I make an effort to prioritize those practices that are most beneficial for me during that particular phase of my life. What is working for me and what isn't? What behaviours do I want to practice to support my current goals?

Without yoga practice, I would unlikely still be able to play basketball at my age. Yoga and proper stretching have surely helped me avoid injury. Before I made yoga a regular practice, my body was in a lot of pain the day after intense sports activity. I would often get little nagging injuries. I also used to suffer from back pain. The same is true of meditation. I notice when I go through a period where I don't take the time to meditate regularly, my emotions are more erratic. I am more stressed or easily frustrated, staying focussed is more difficult, and I can become overwhelmed by my thoughts. I know these practices are important, so I make them a priority.

Priorities may change depending on your circumstances and the goals you are trying to achieve. Clarity is important when setting priorities, and your philosophy can help you gain more clarity. Is what I am spending my time on getting me closer to the life that I want?

Remember, priorities are what you make time for over anything else you want to do. Habit number three in Stephen Covey's *Seven Habits of Highly Effective People* is Put first things first. It's age-old advice but even more relevant now as the pace of life seems to be increasing along with the number of distractions we face.

Measurement and Reflection

When I start working with a new coaching client, I like to try to help them measure where they are currently, both to define our starting point and to allow us to measure their progress. I use what is called the "Wheel of Life." This is basically a large circle on a page divided into eight equal pieces, like a pie or a pizza. At the top of each section on the outer edge of the circle, a heading defining an area of life is written, such as health, relationships, or career. Within each section or pie shape, you can rate your current satisfaction with that part of your life named in the heading. I tell people to rate these on a scale of zero to ten, marking a ten if it can't get any better or zero if it can't get any worse. When the chart is complete, it can assess what parts of your life you are happy with and which need changes.

When you measure where you are at any given point in your life, it allows you to come back to it months or years later. Reflecting on where you were in the past and how far you have come can be motivating and inspiring. If you haven't made any progress or things have gotten worse, it can be a wake-up call that change is overdue or your strategies are not working.

According to the writings of Plato, Socrates is said to have claimed, "An unexamined life is not worth living." The phrase "ignorance is bliss" comes from a poem by English poet Thomas Gray. Both ideas have merit, but taken to extremes, both can be a detrimental part of your philosophy. Regularly examining your life and reflecting on your beliefs and actions is clearly something I believe in quite strongly, considering the premise of this book. However, overanalyzing and micromanaging your life can cause paralysis in your ability to act. Conversely, how many people would not have started on a journey to pursue a goal if they had known how difficult it would be?

Reflection is not just the evaluation and analysis of events in your life. It can be the act of checking in with your body to see what it needs. We often avoid listening to our bodies until something goes wrong. Reflecting on our emotional state will also help us understand our spiritual needs or deep unconscious desires. As you learn to reflect on external events and internal experiences, the way to a more fulfilling life will become apparent, and with it, more moments of happiness.

Final Thoughts

Much like happiness, success is not a destination. There are rarely moments where we suddenly realize we are successful. Success is something that develops over time as you make small improvements daily. It comes through developing the right practices.

The philosophy that I have described is what I aspire to. It is not something I can claim to live without fail. When I live in alignment with these principles, I feel happier and my life flows in a more harmonious way. I am also confident it has led to the level of success that I have enjoyed in many areas of my life. It's not easy, but it's worth it.

"The road to these things that I have pointed out now seems very hard, but it can be found. And of course something that is found so rarely is bound to be hard. For if salvation were ready to hand and could be found without great effort, how could it come about that almost everyone neglects it? But excellence is as difficult as it is rare."
- Spinoza -

In Buddhism, we are not born with compassion. Compassion is cultivated. I think this is similar to the way we develop our values and beliefs. We may define our values at a young age, but it takes time to practice this behaviour and learn to manage the fears that keep us from it. A philosophy that does not evolve is dogma. As we experience life, we can gain new insights and broaden our understanding. Remaining tied to old beliefs and perspectives will interfere with your evolution on a mental and emotional level.

It's important to be discerning with what you believe, but be patient with people's advice and assume good intentions, even if their ideas do not fit your philosophy. American poet and Pulitzer Prize winner Mary Oliver has wise words for us:

"Let me keep my distance, always, from those who think they have the answers. Let me keep company always with those who say "Look!" and laugh in astonishment, and bow their heads."

I began this book by emphasizing the importance of happiness. To support this happiness, I have encouraged you to review your beliefs to help you recognize where revisions are needed. However, knowing what you need to be happy is not enough. To highlight this point, I will share one more story with you. Christopher Boyce spent decades on academic research to better understand what makes people happy. Despite his ability to rationally understand happiness, he was no closer to it himself until he quit his job and began cycling through different parts of the world, ending up in the Himalayan mountain kingdom of Bhutan. It was on this journey that he experienced what it means to be happy. If your philosophy does not help you create the experiences that make you happy, perhaps you are not truly living it.

Even if you are not convinced that a philosophy focussed on authentic happiness can bring out a person's highest potential, I hope I have encouraged you to become more aware of your beliefs. Moreover, I hope you have become convinced of the importance of philosophy and the awareness of the beliefs that pervade our societies. Human beings have developed rational thought to a degree that we have been able to develop amazing technologies, and yet so many of our social issues persist. As a species, we have come so far in terms of intelligence, but in many ways, we are still in our infancy, where our spiritual/emotional development is concerned. If all we needed were more intelligence or computational power, we would not have an epidemic of depression and other mental health issues in the most technically developed countries of the world. Our cultural norms and the beliefs that drive them, our collective habits of thought and action—these are the things that will save us or destroy us.

It may not be possible for me to create collective change in society's beliefs, but such beliefs will be challenged or carefully considered over time by new generations. Perhaps a more conscious awareness of beliefs on an individual level will contribute to positive change within communities or even in our collective consciousness. Whatever you believe, I hope I have encouraged you to become more aware of the beliefs that do not serve you and to develop the courage to change them.

"Now is the time to get serious about living your ideals.
Once you have determined the spiritual principles you wish to exemplify,
abide by these rules as if they were laws, as if it were indeed sinful to compromise
them. Don't mind if others don't share your convictions. How long can you afford
to put off who you really want to be? Your nobler self cannot wait any longer."
- Epictetus -

Questions
• What has become clearer to you with the ideas you have read?
• How do you define a good life? What can you do each day to live that good life?

- Do you have any particular goals after reading this book?
- What practices will you commit to going forward? How will your practices support your goals?

ABOUT THE AUTHOR

Peter Teuscher was born in Germany in 1967. At the age of four, he moved to Canada with his mother and stepfather, where he grew up and lived until he was 35. In 2002 he left Canada and travelled through Asia followed by the start of a new life in Europe. It was the beginning of a journey of self-discovery and personal development which inspired him to pursue his education as a systemic coach. He has been working as a coach since 2013 and lives in Hamburg, Germany. To find out more about his work you can visit his website www.peterteuscher.com

Made in the USA
Las Vegas, NV
26 April 2024

89151617R00138